Hair Stylist Coloring Book

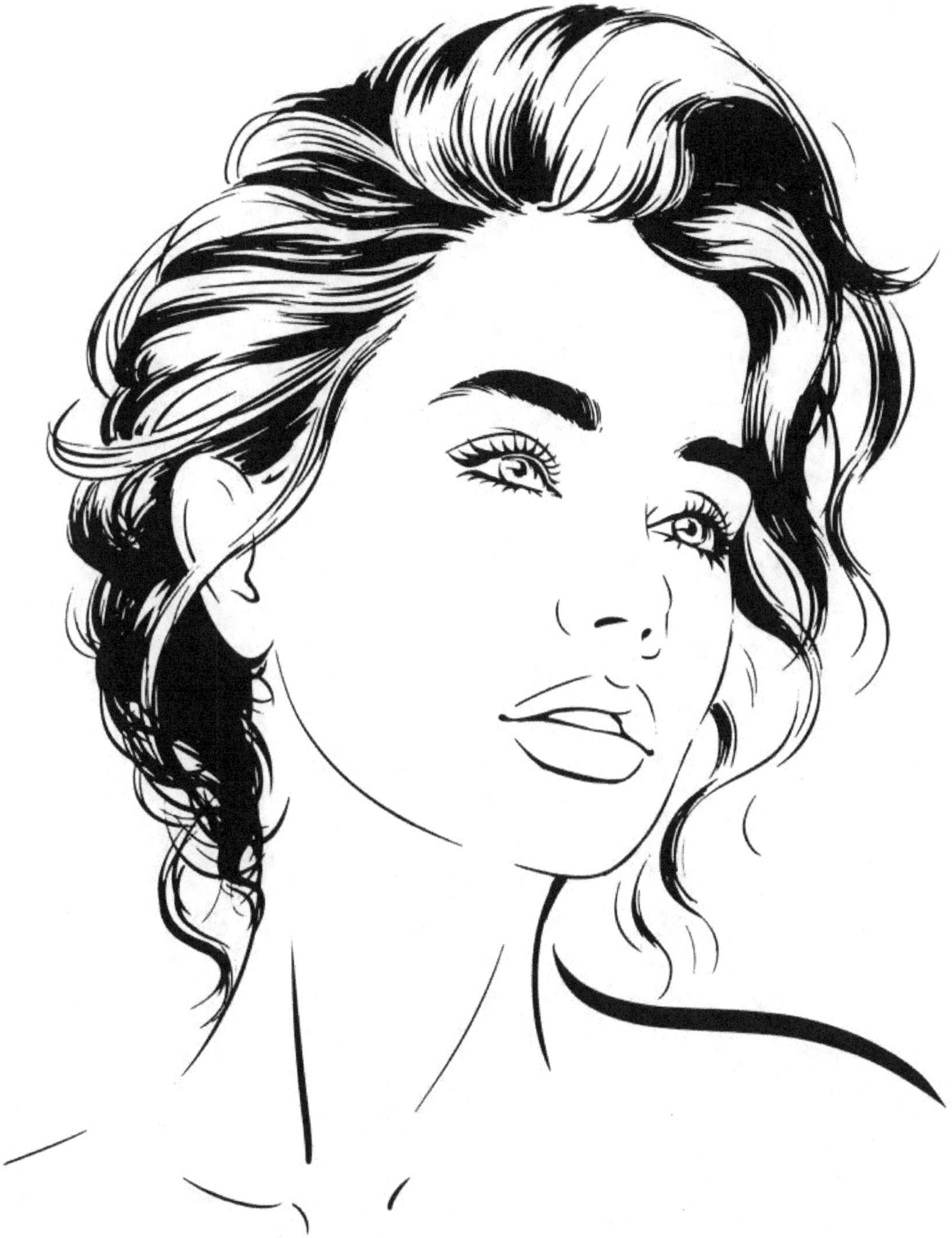

Copyright © 2020 Katrin Stark

ALL RIGHTS RESERVED

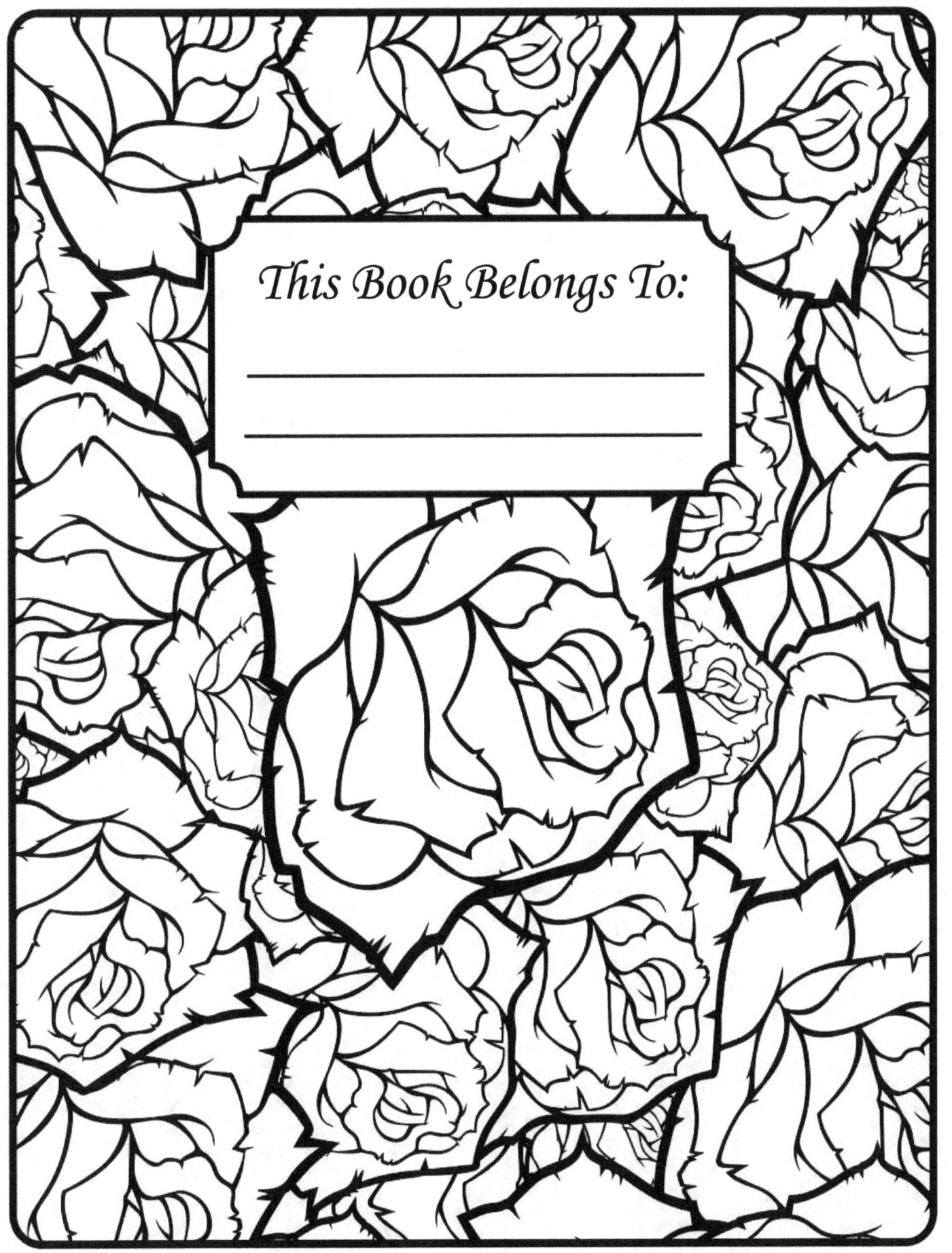

Color Test Page

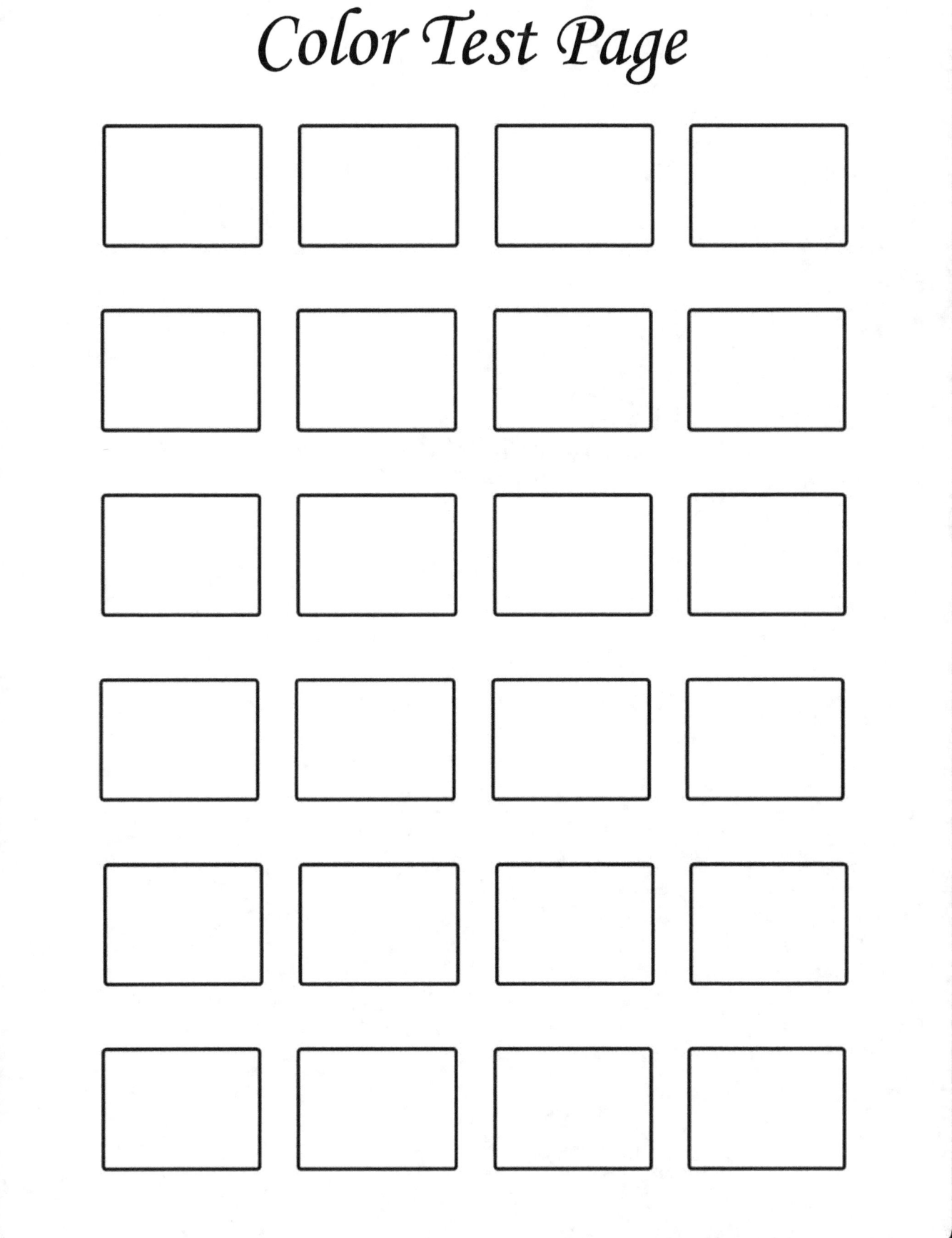

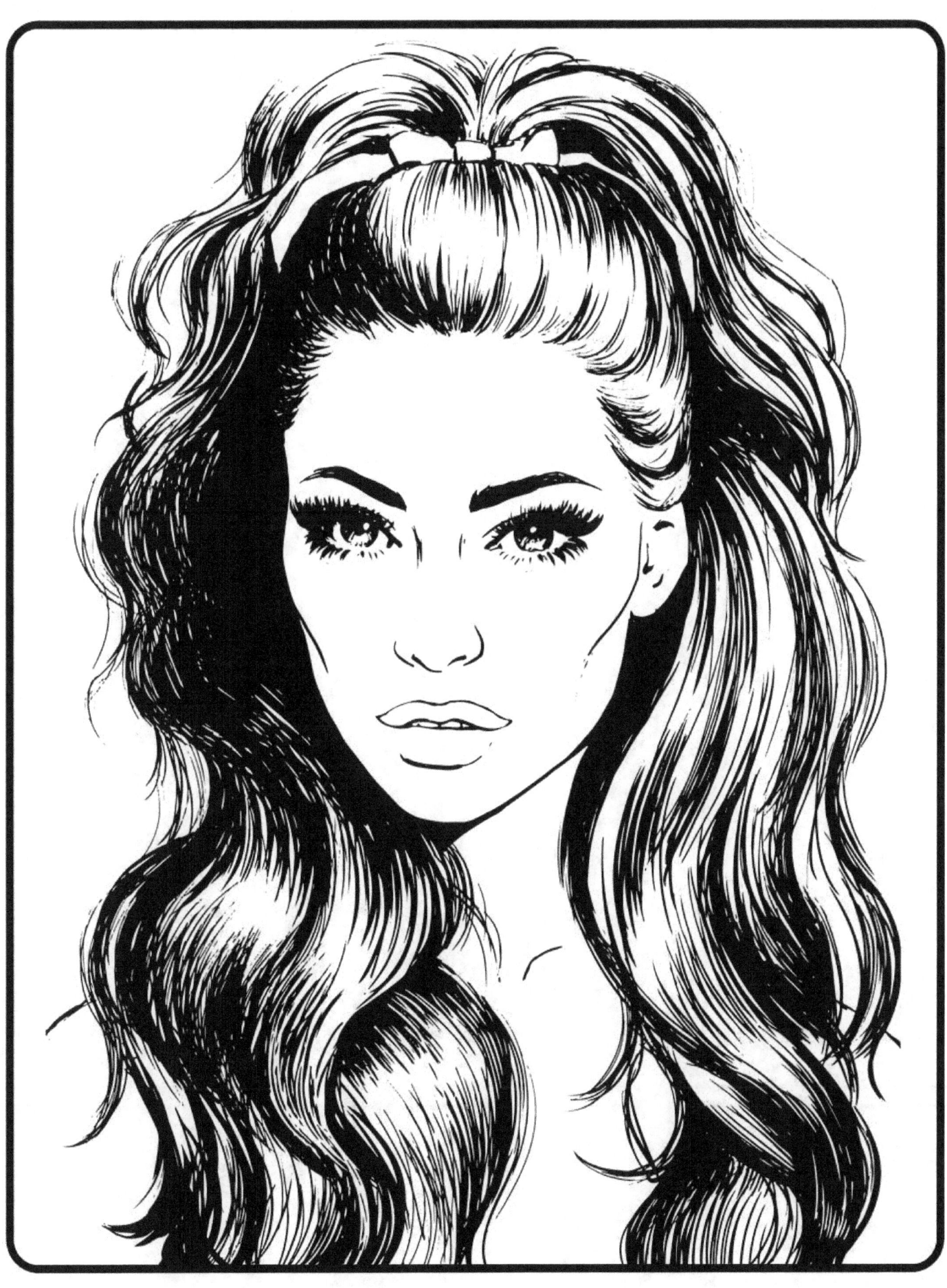

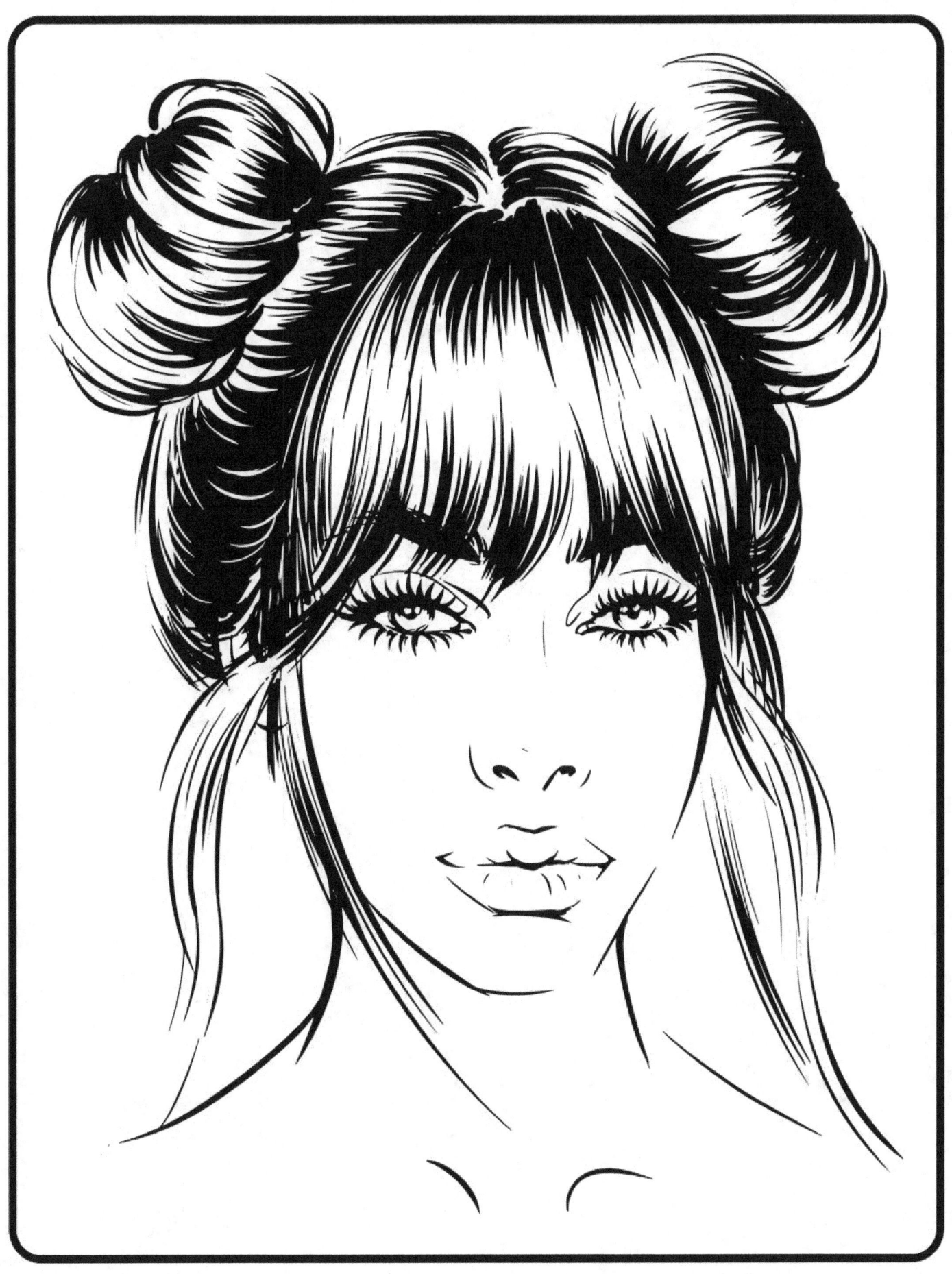

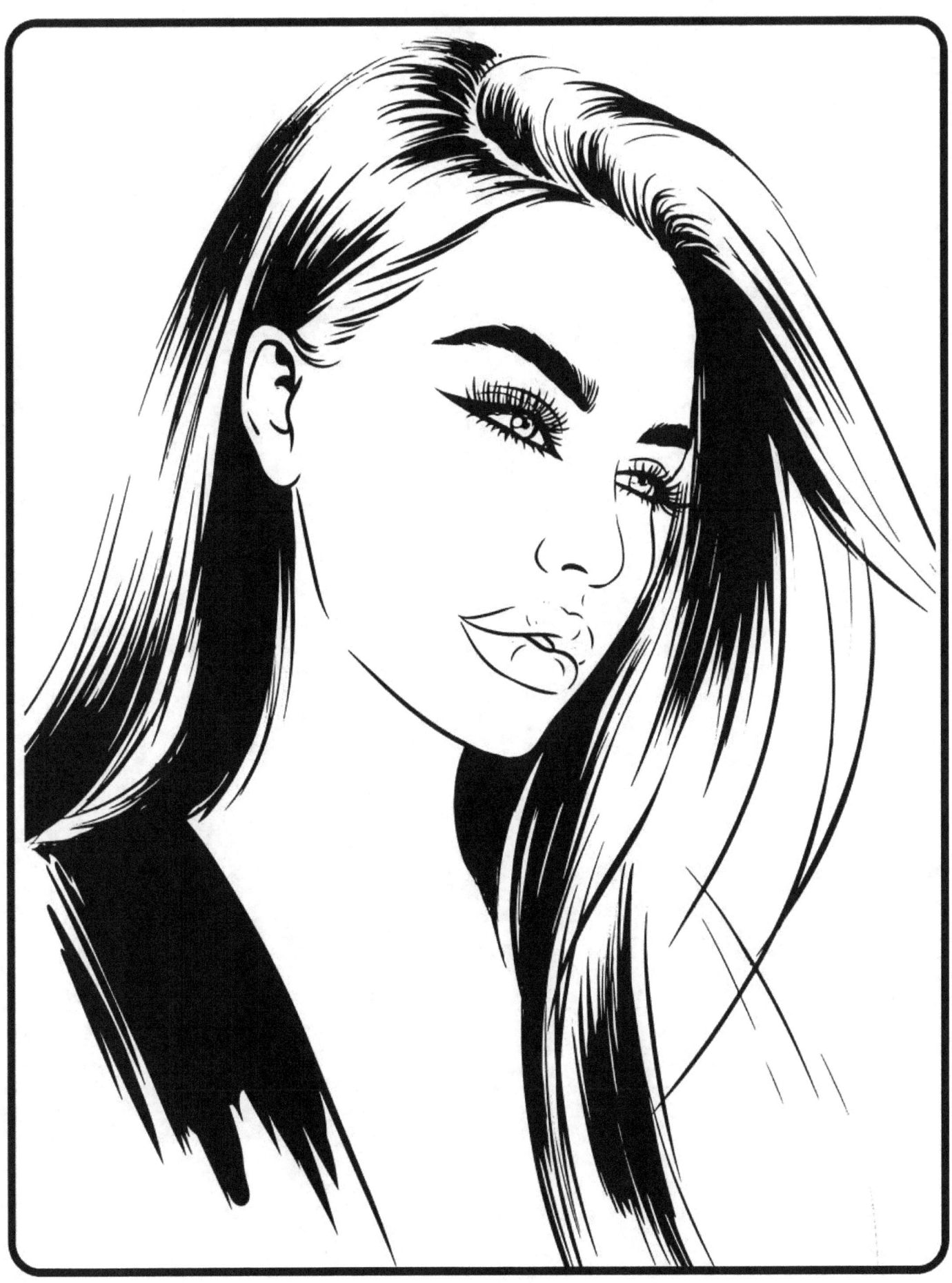

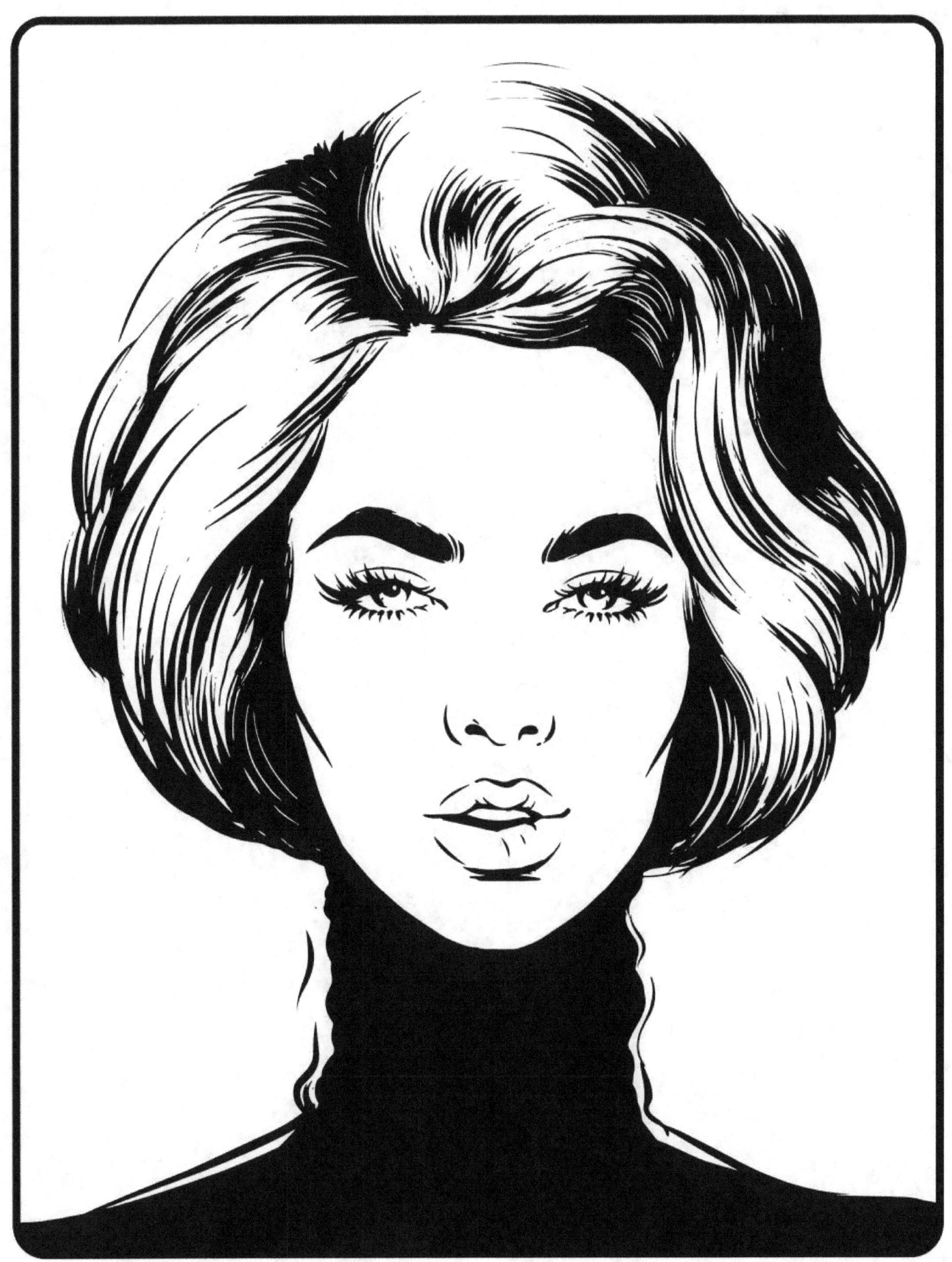

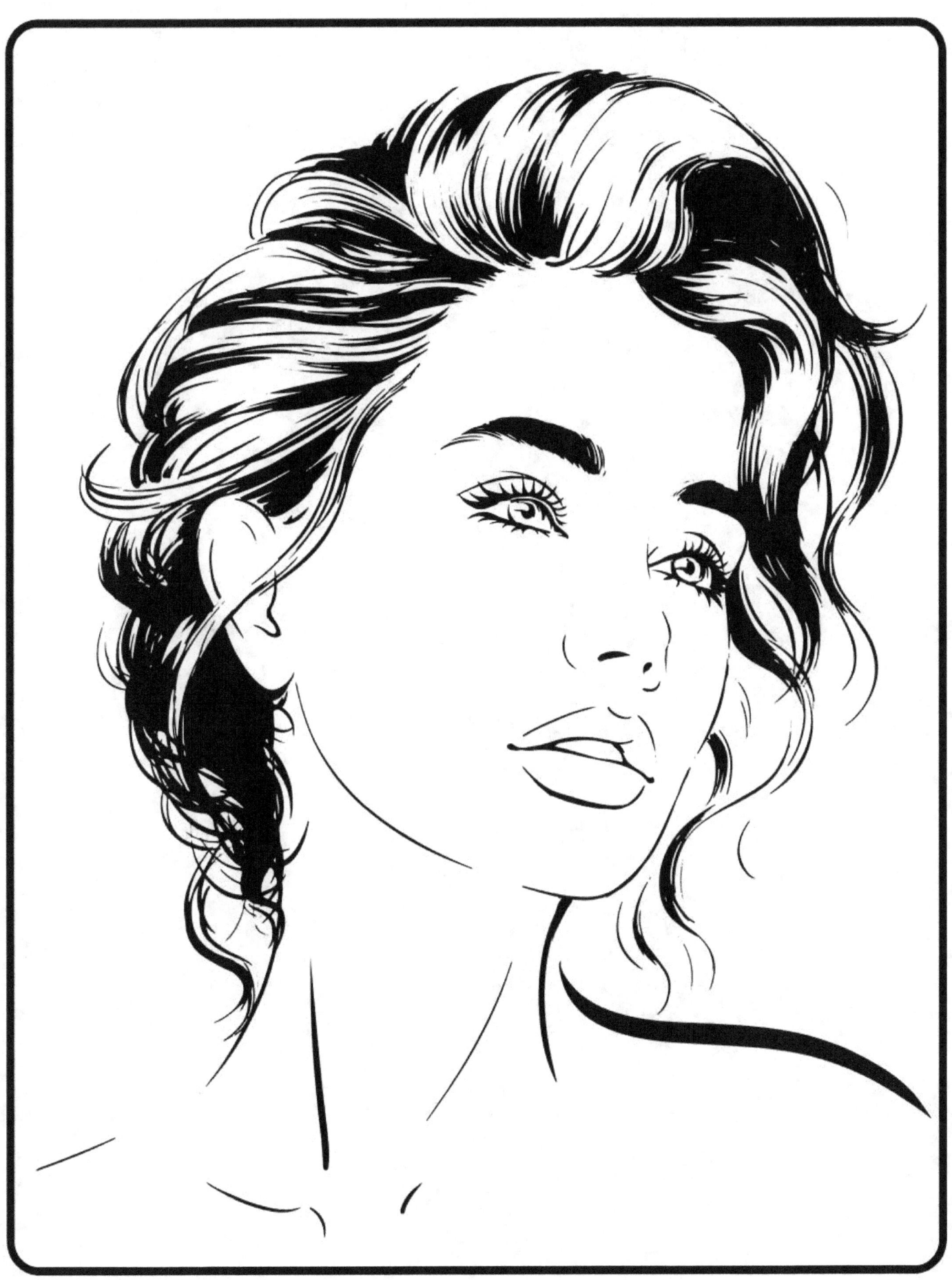

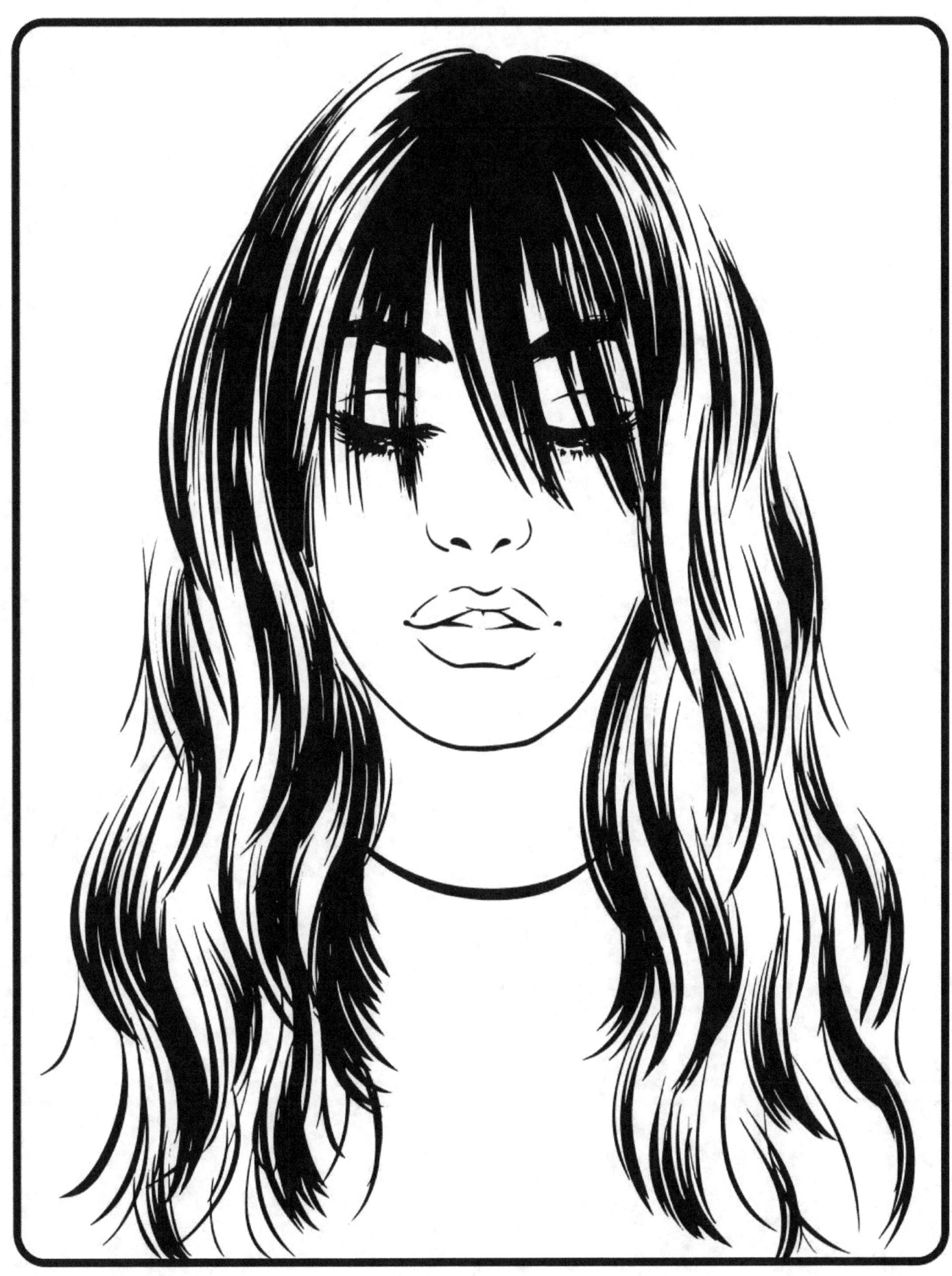

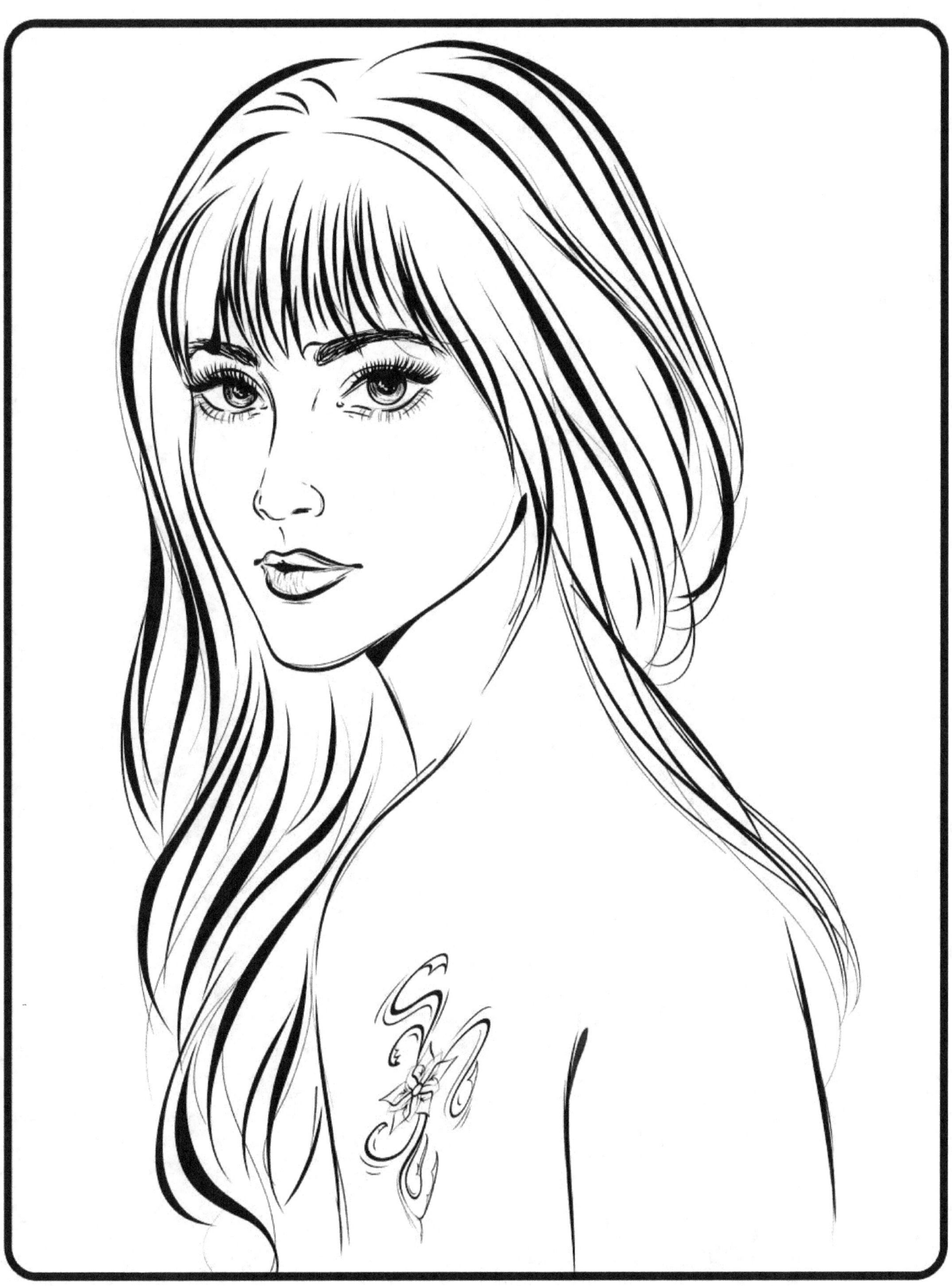

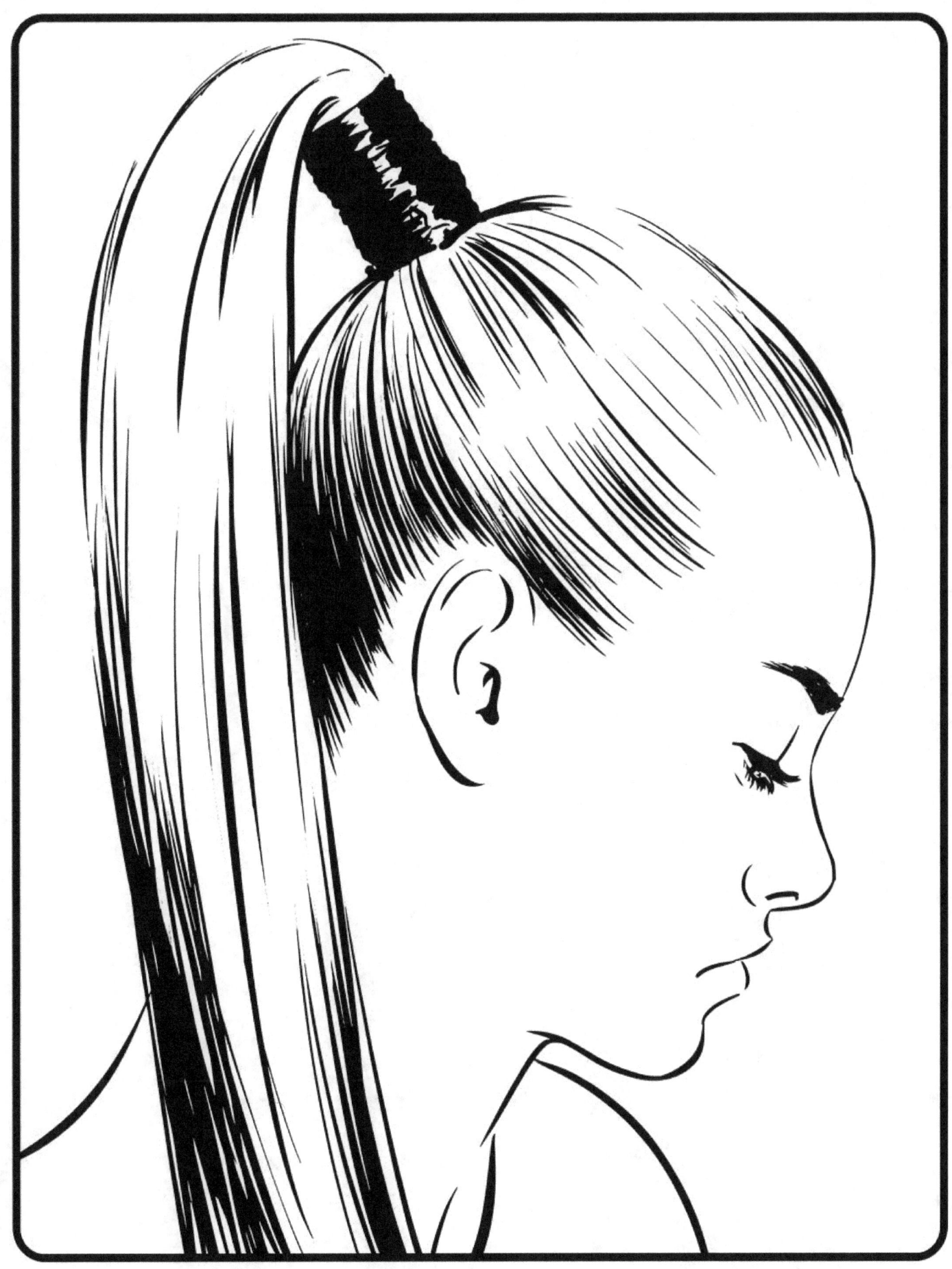

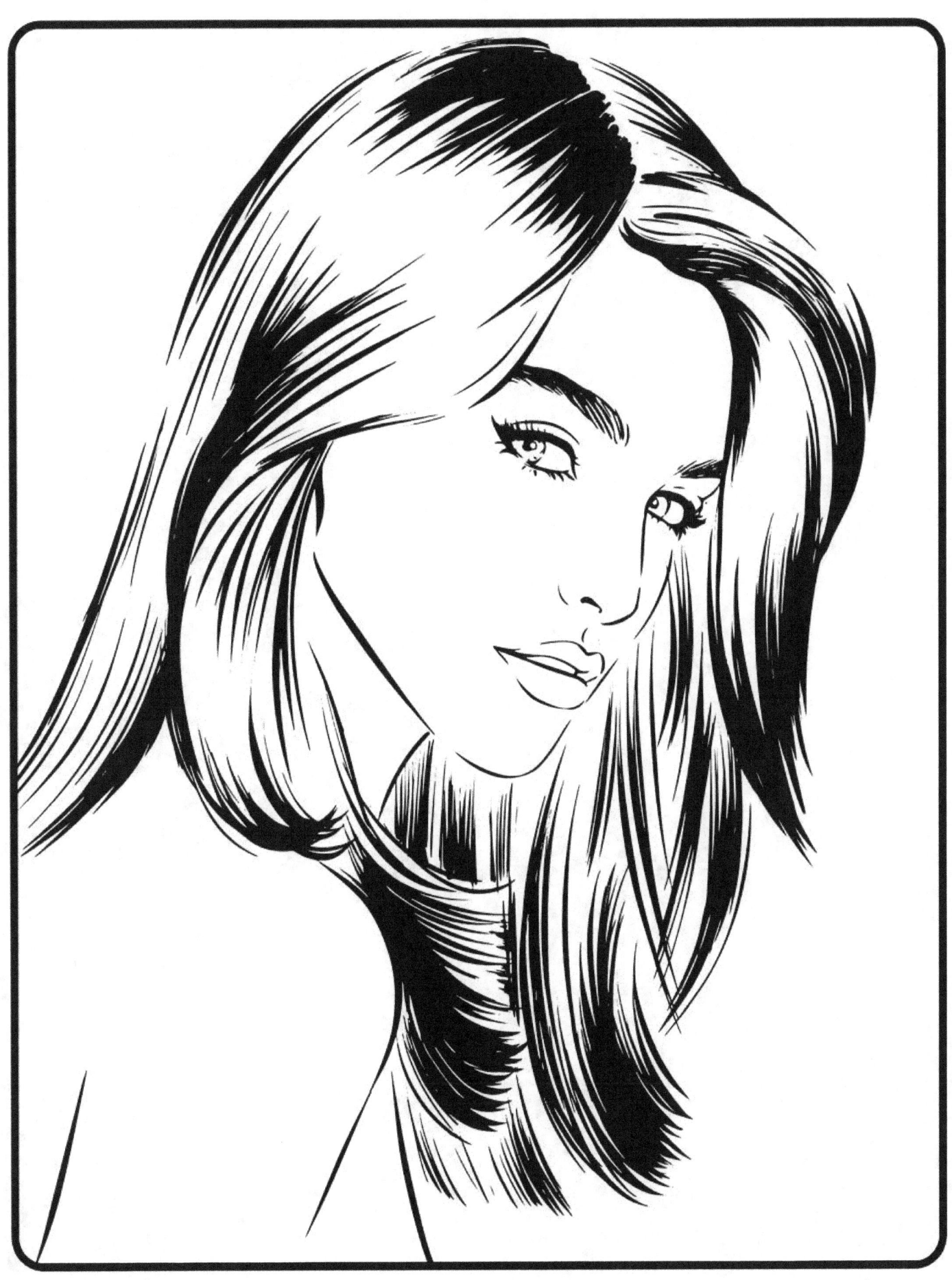

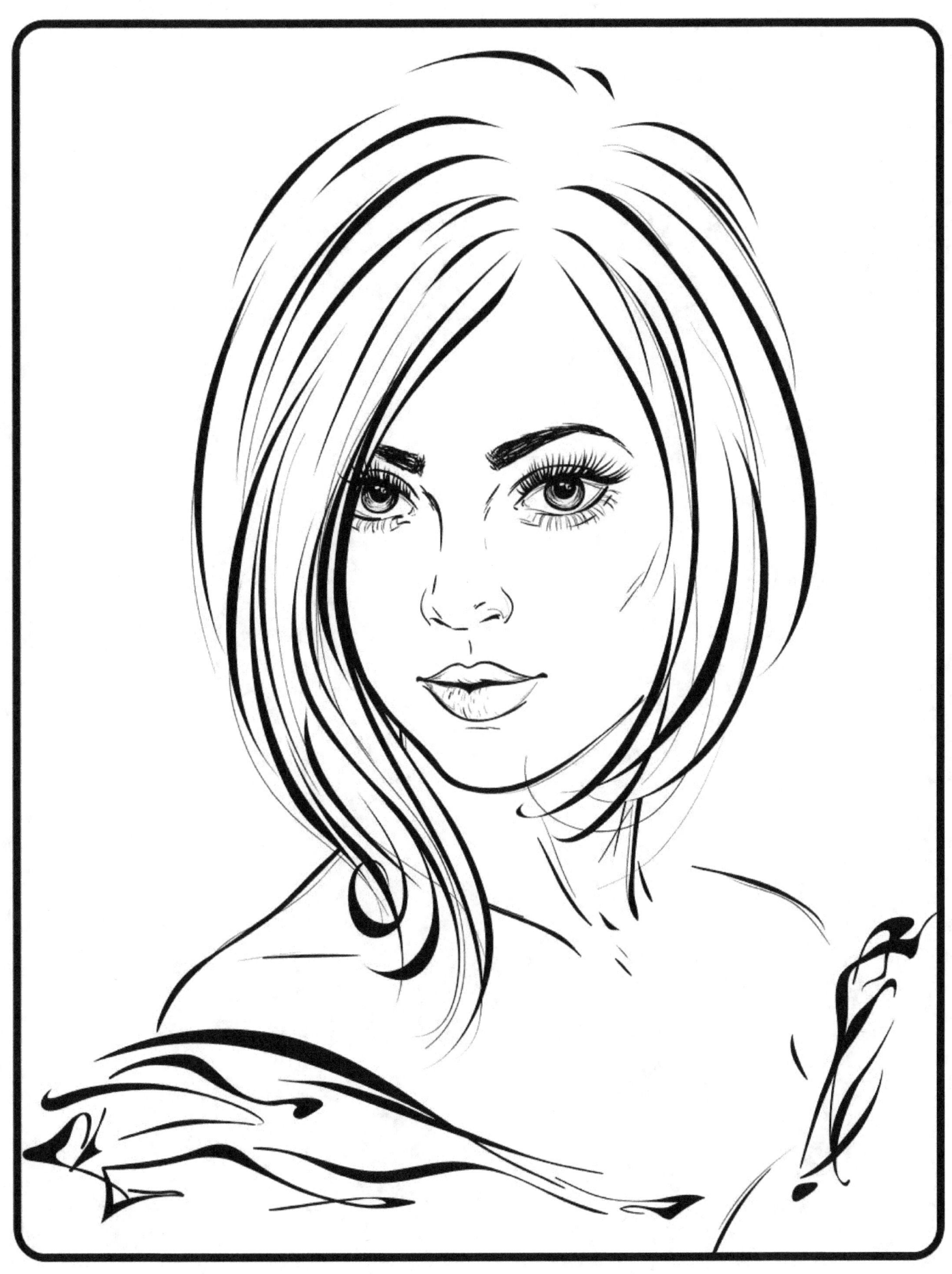

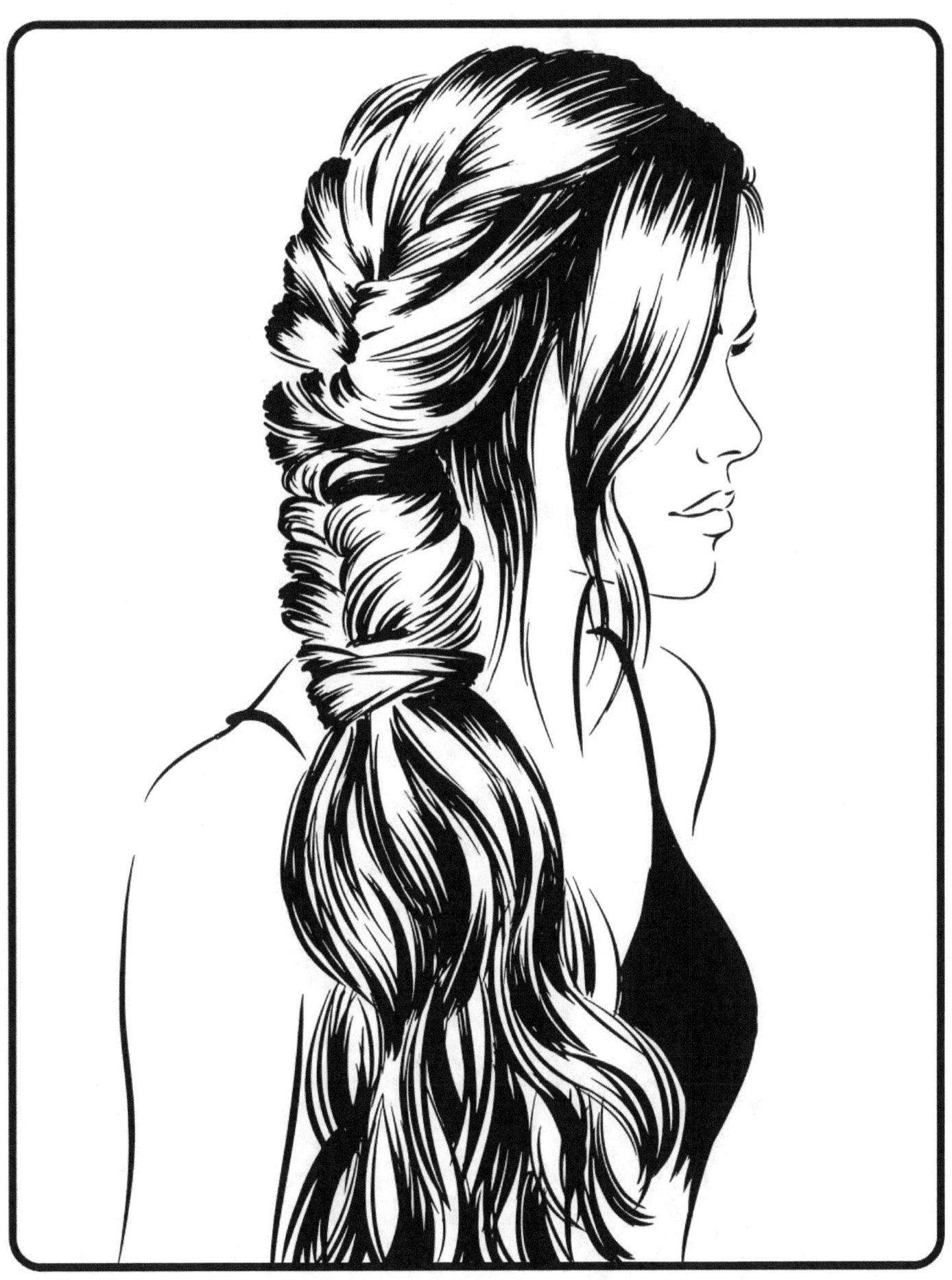

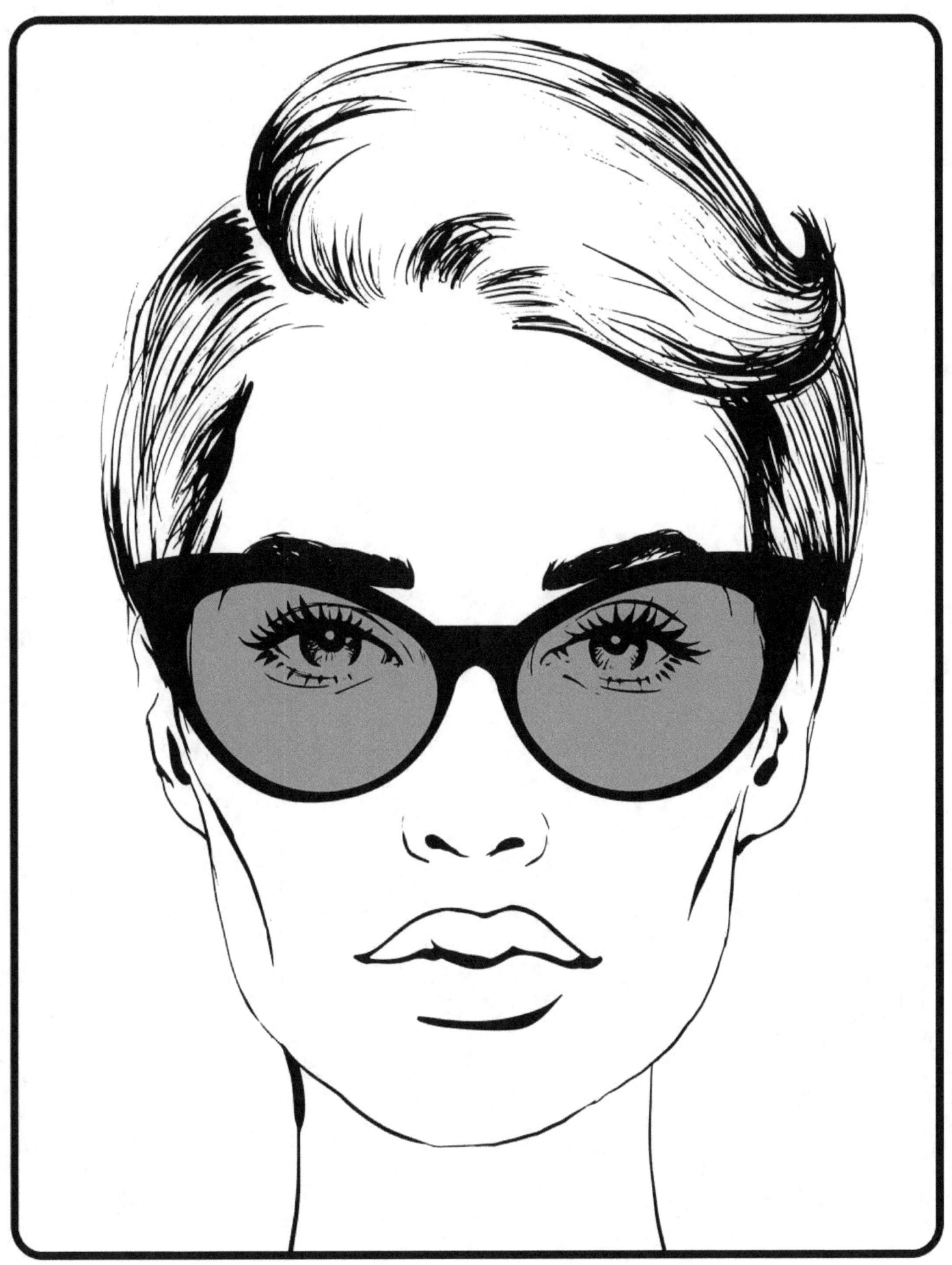

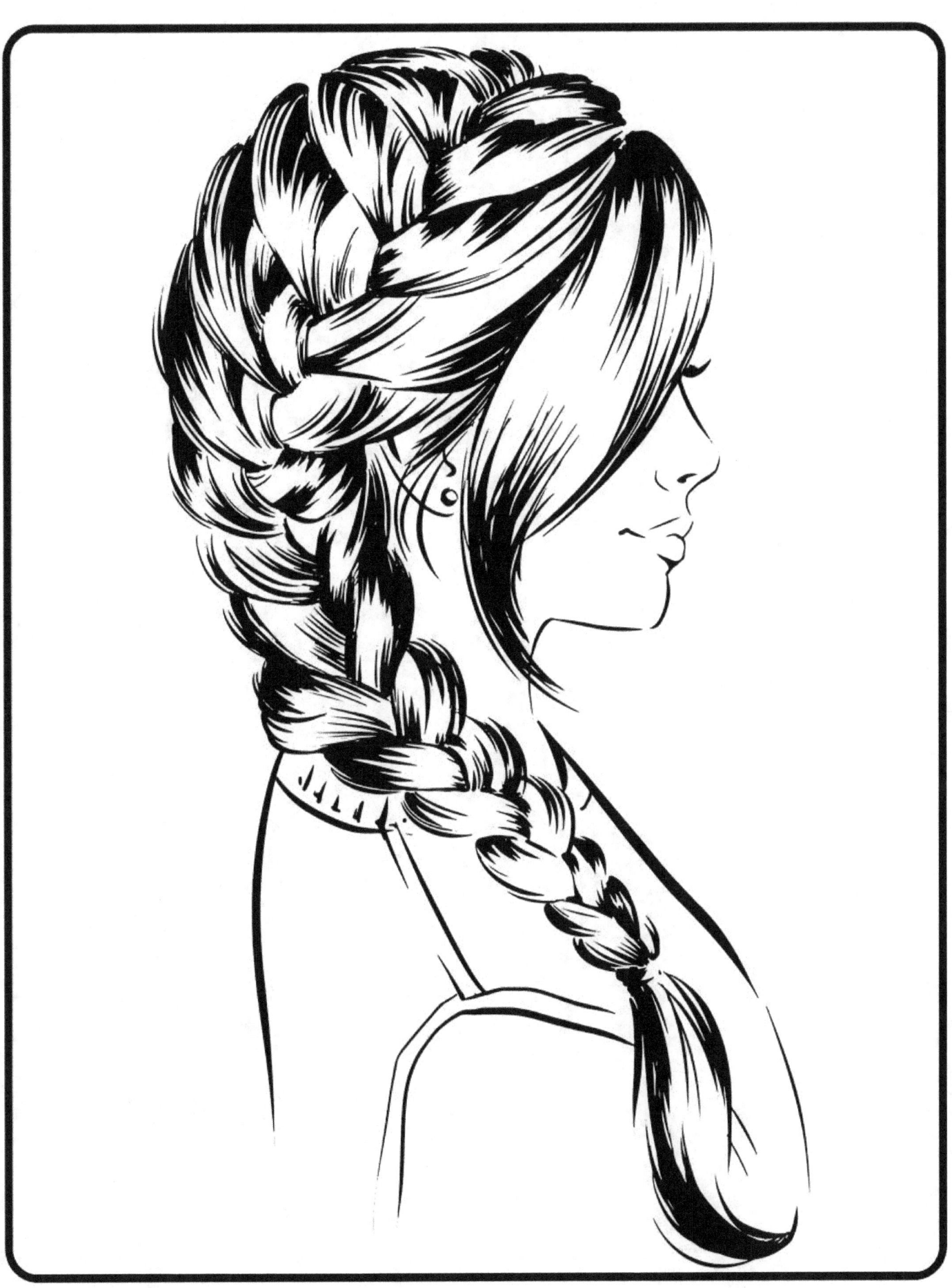

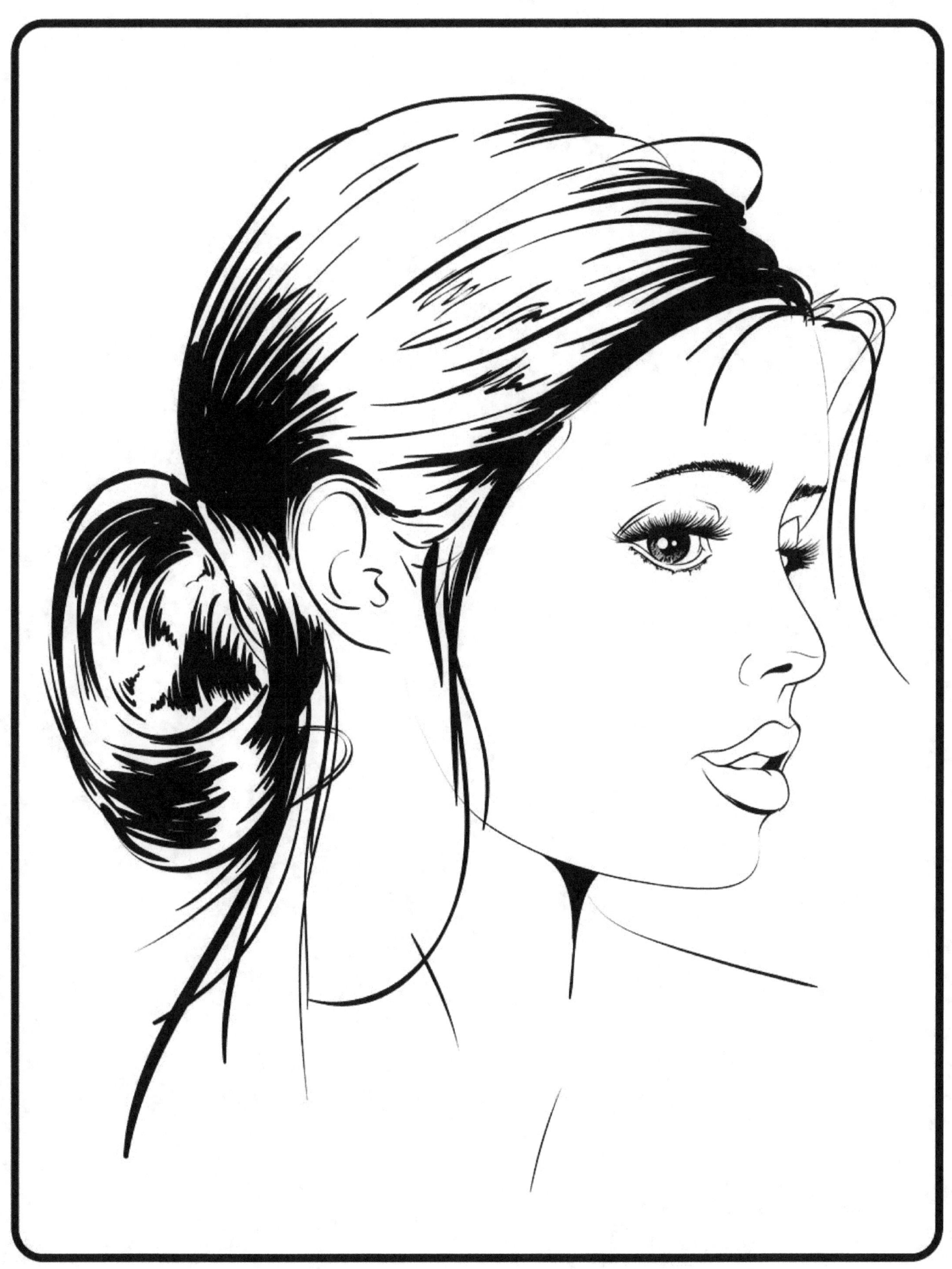

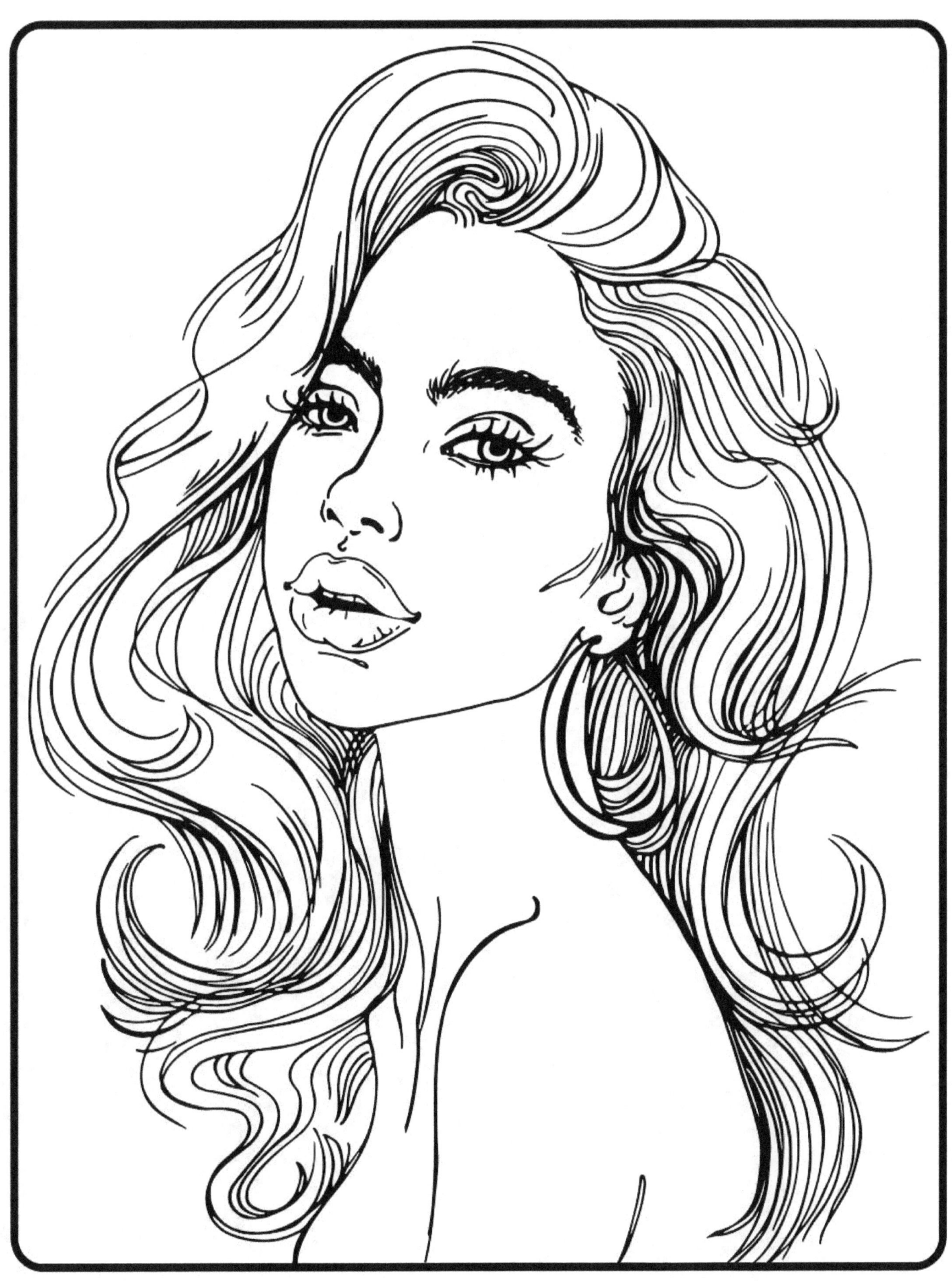

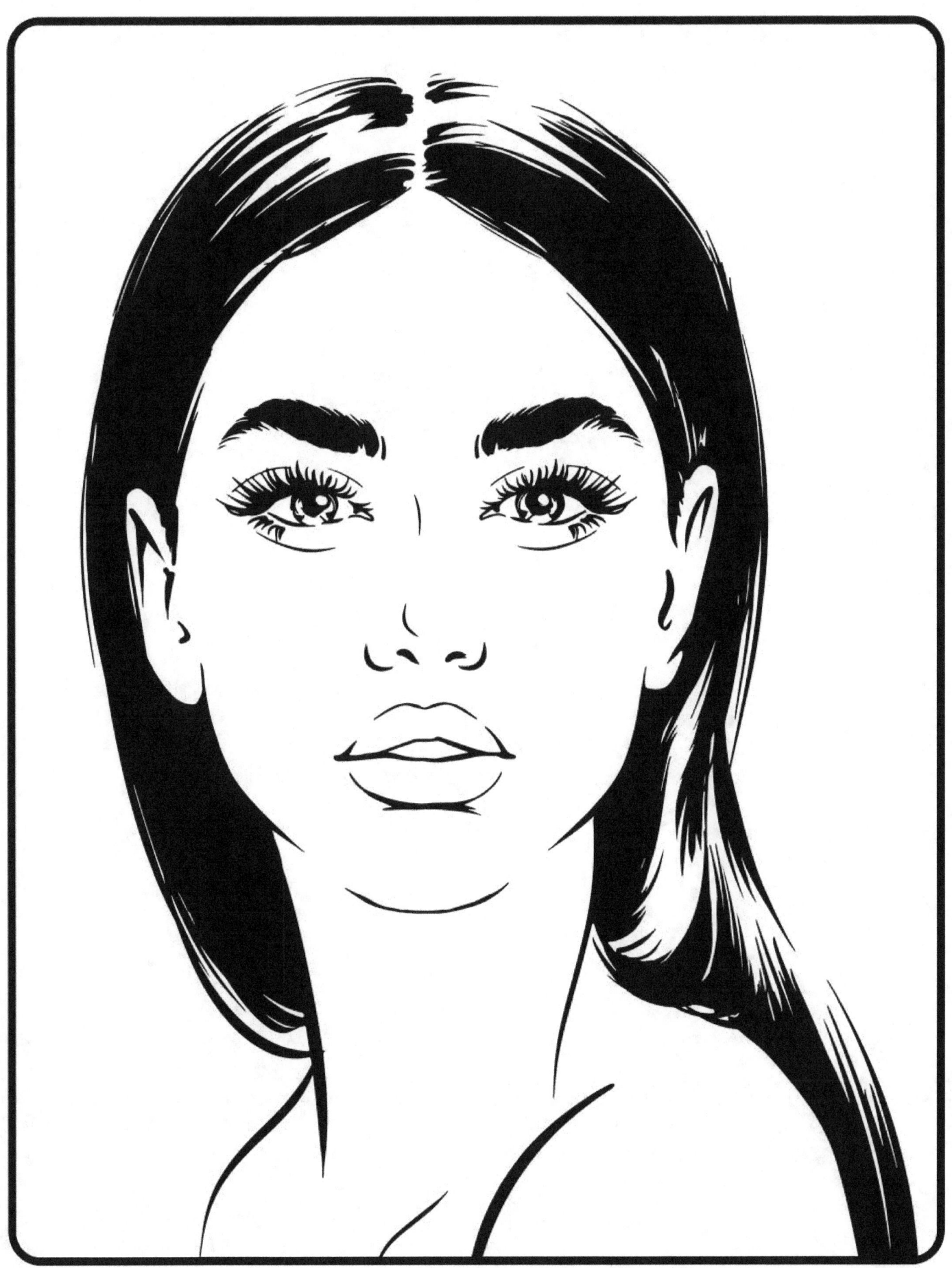

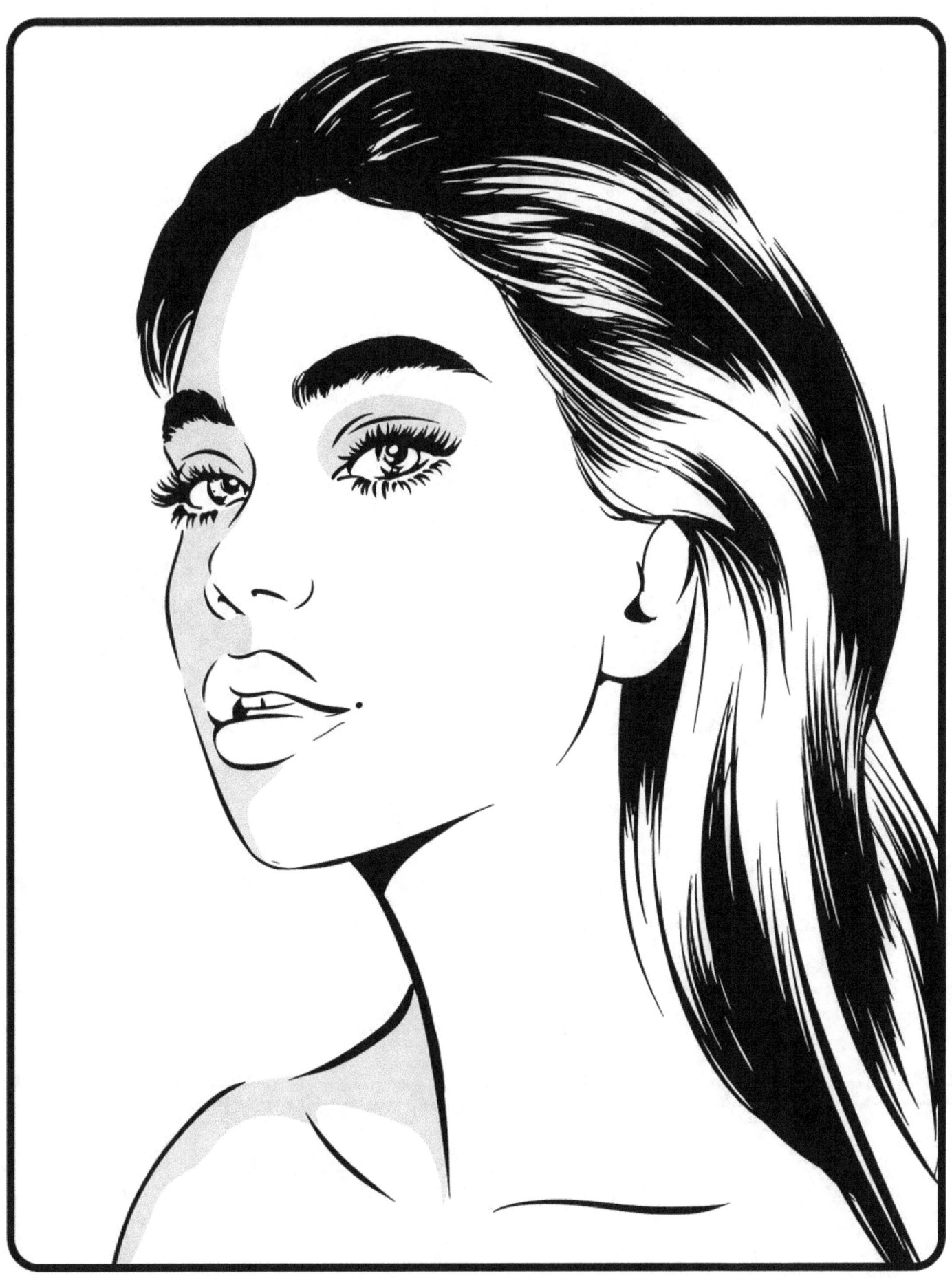

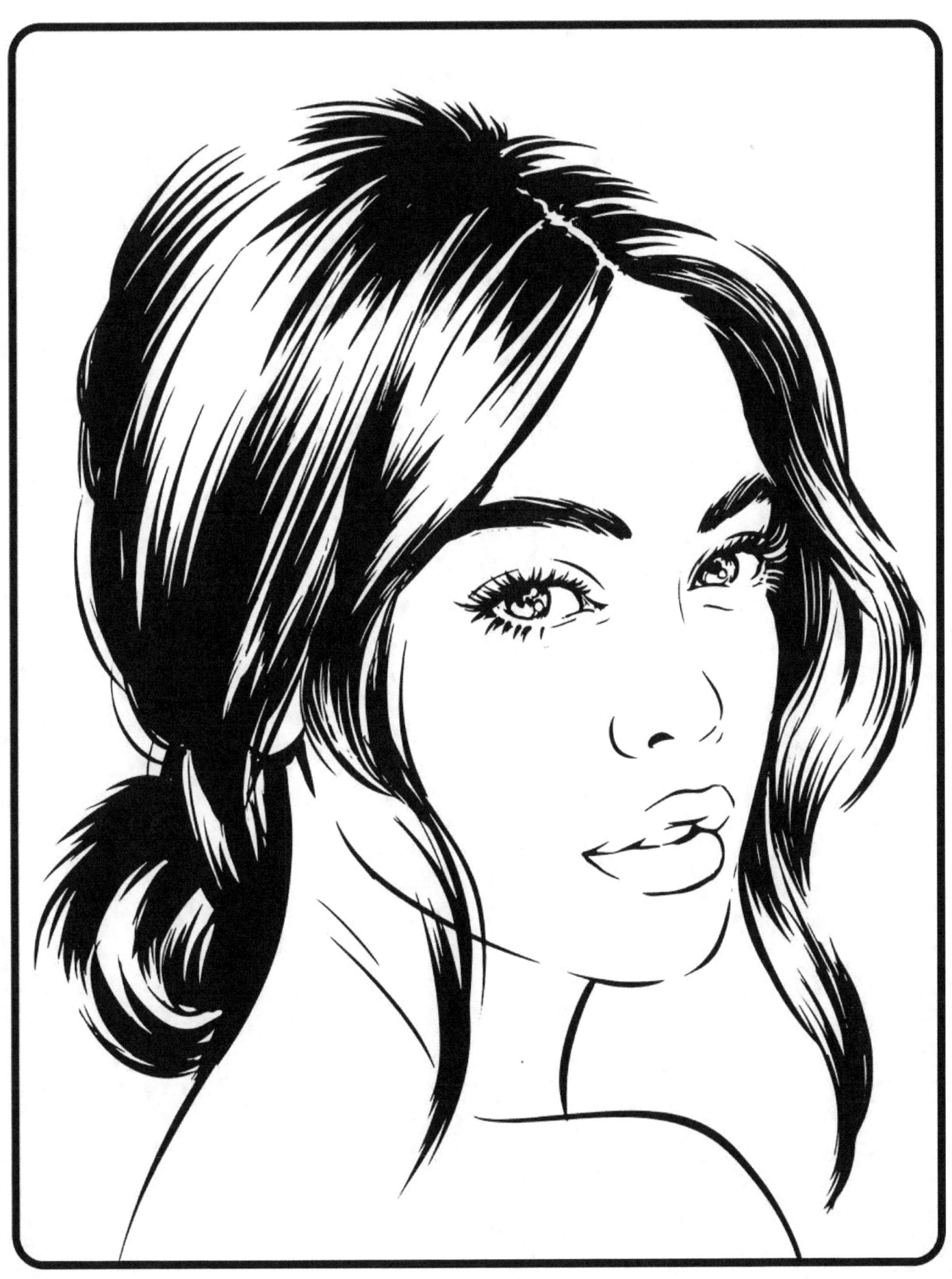

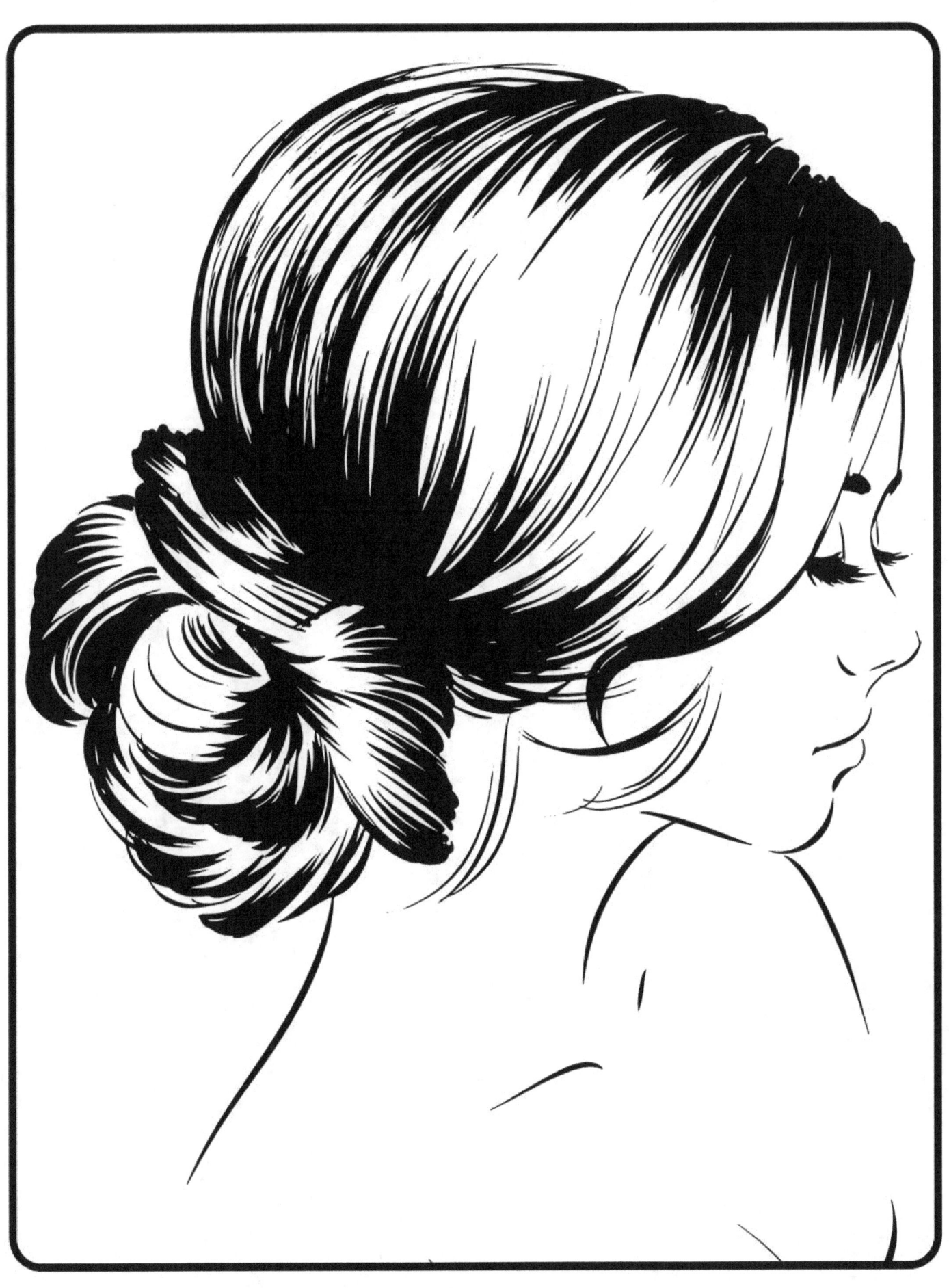

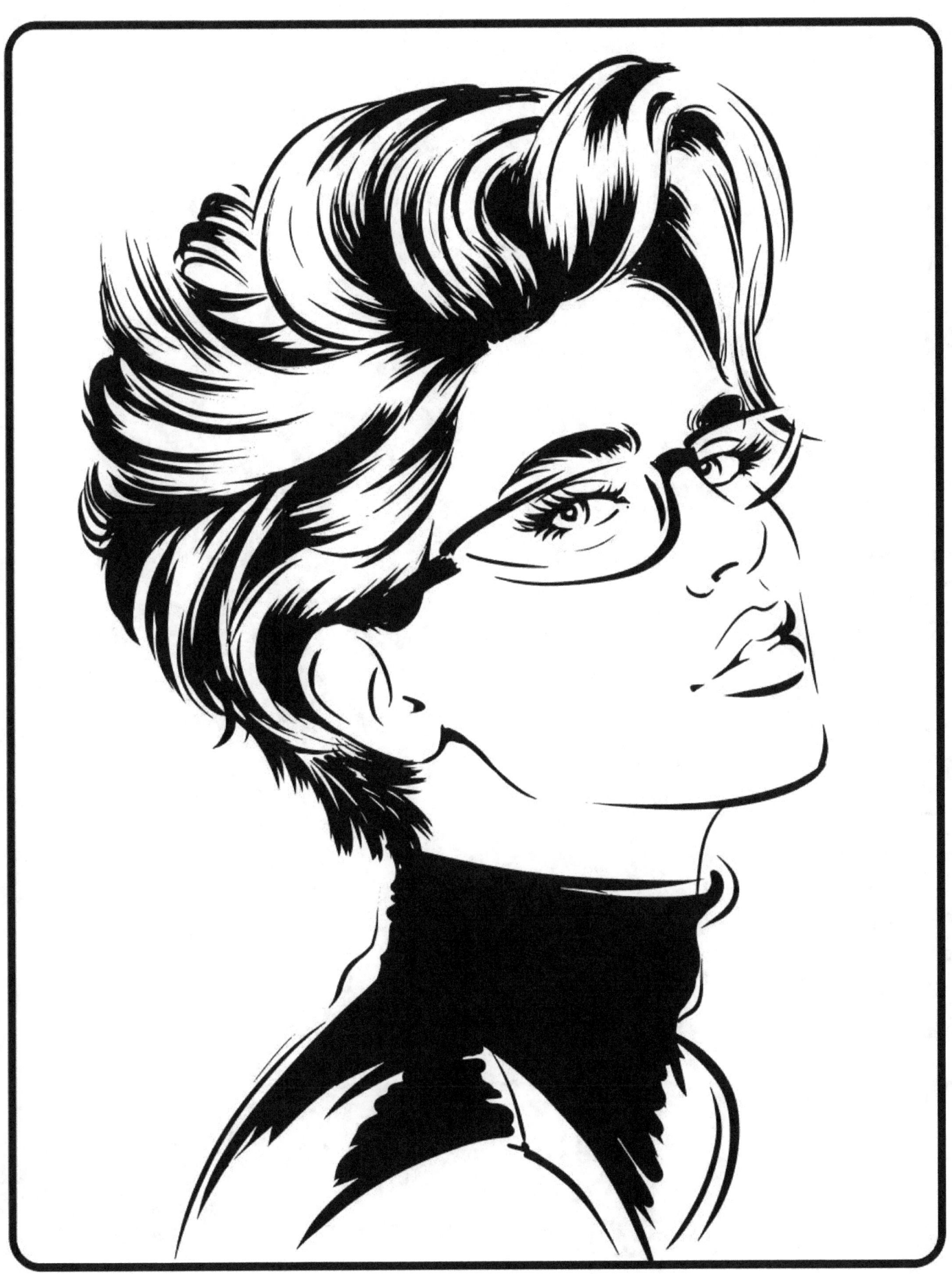

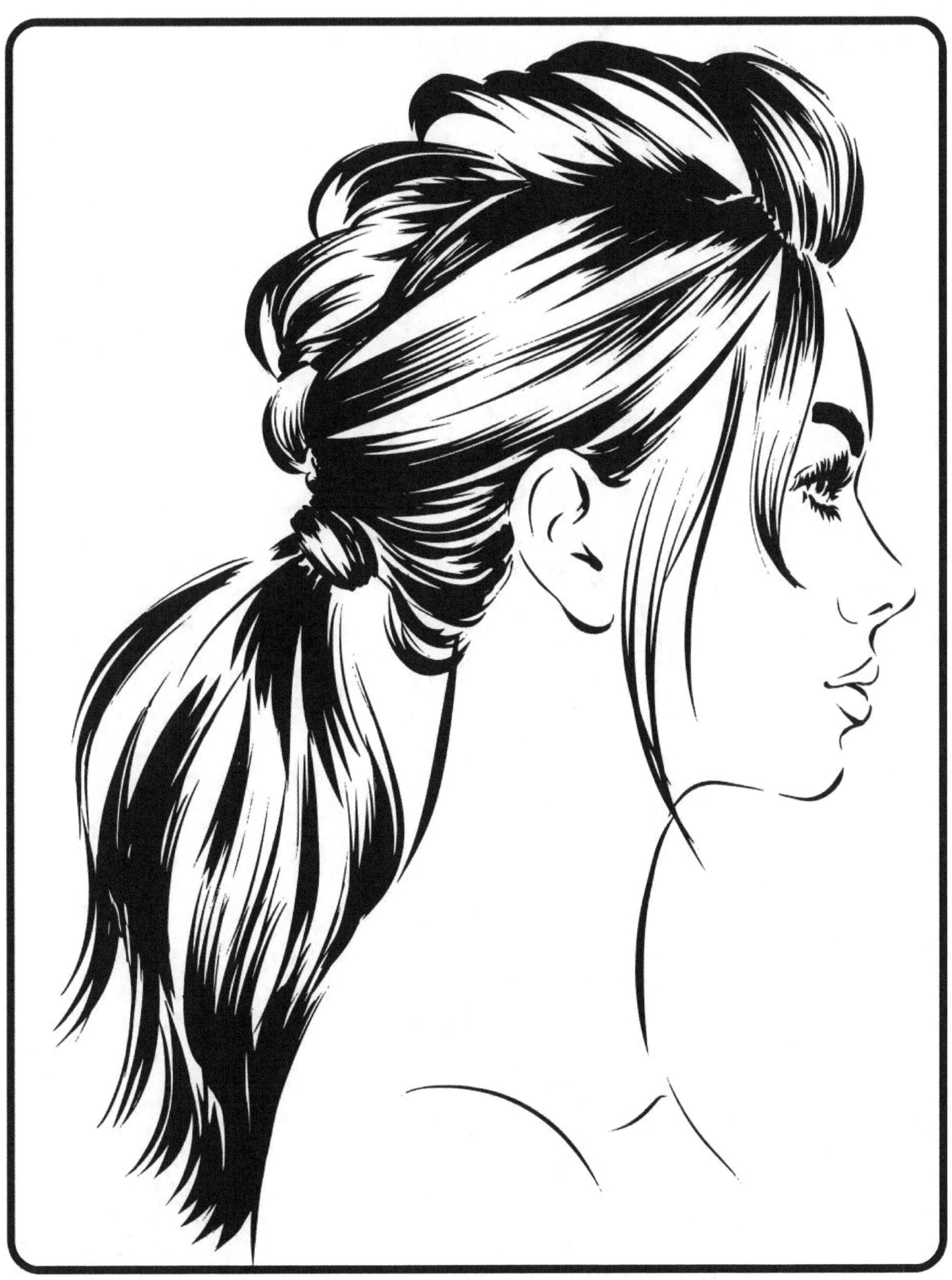

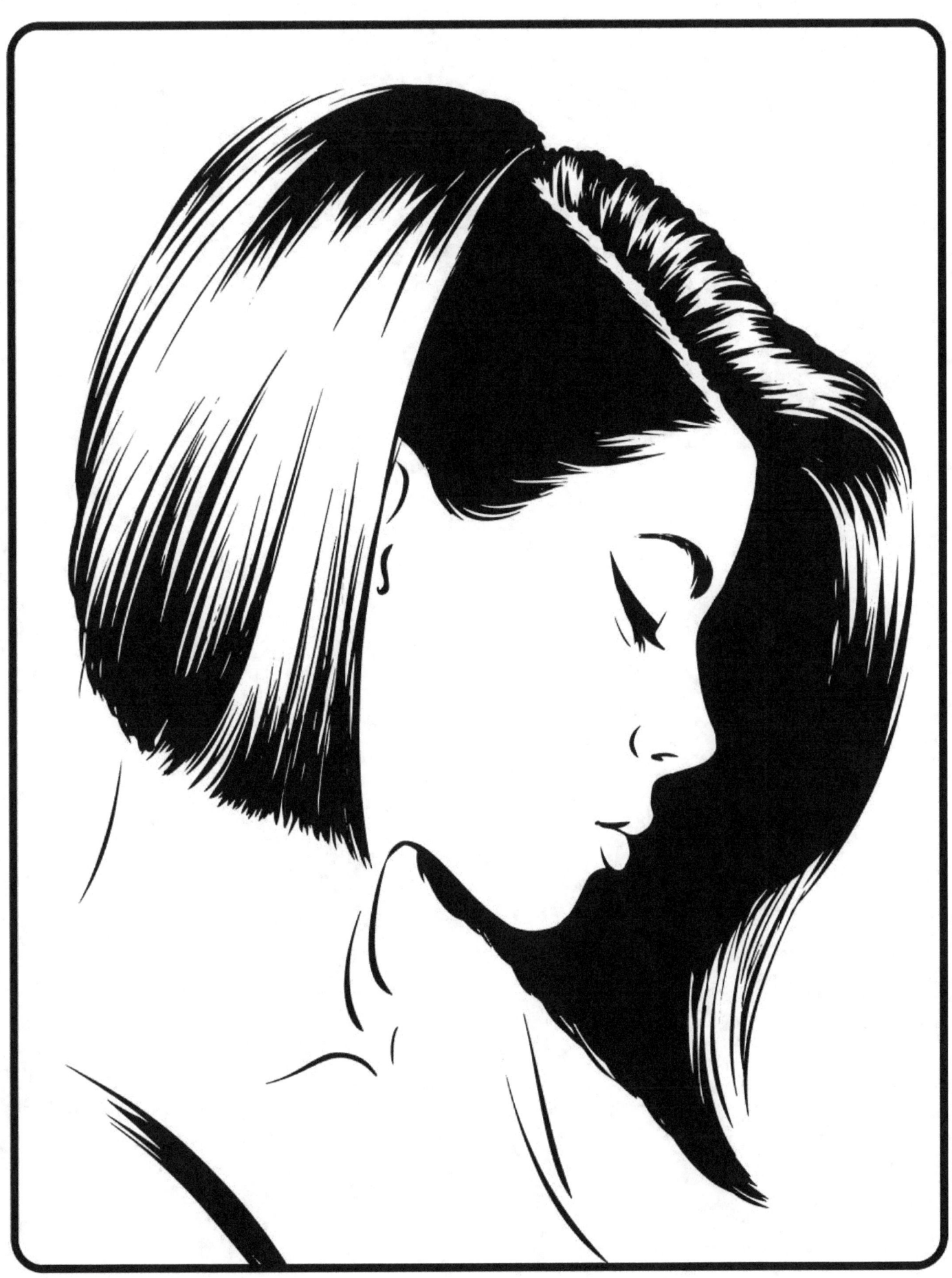

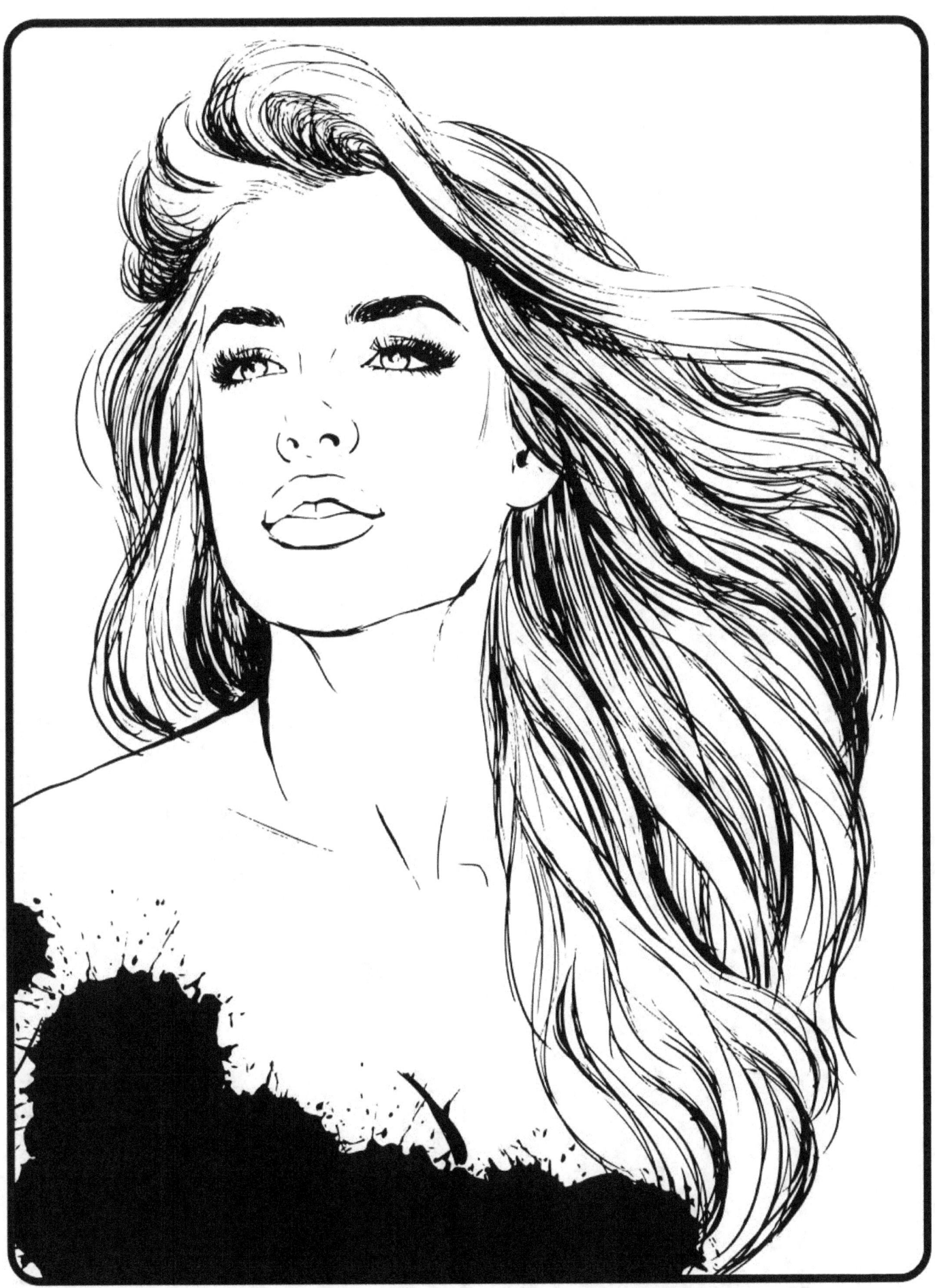

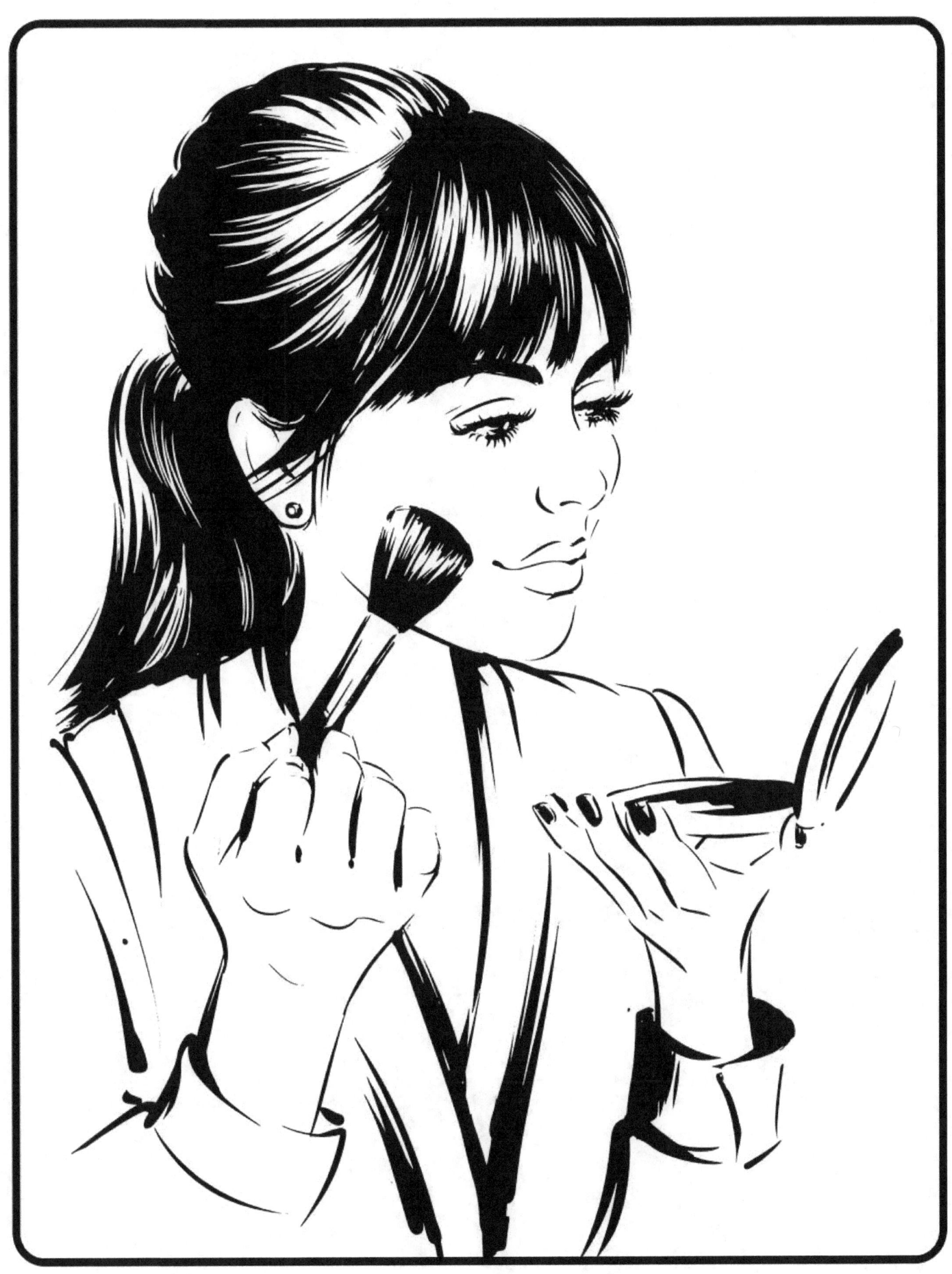

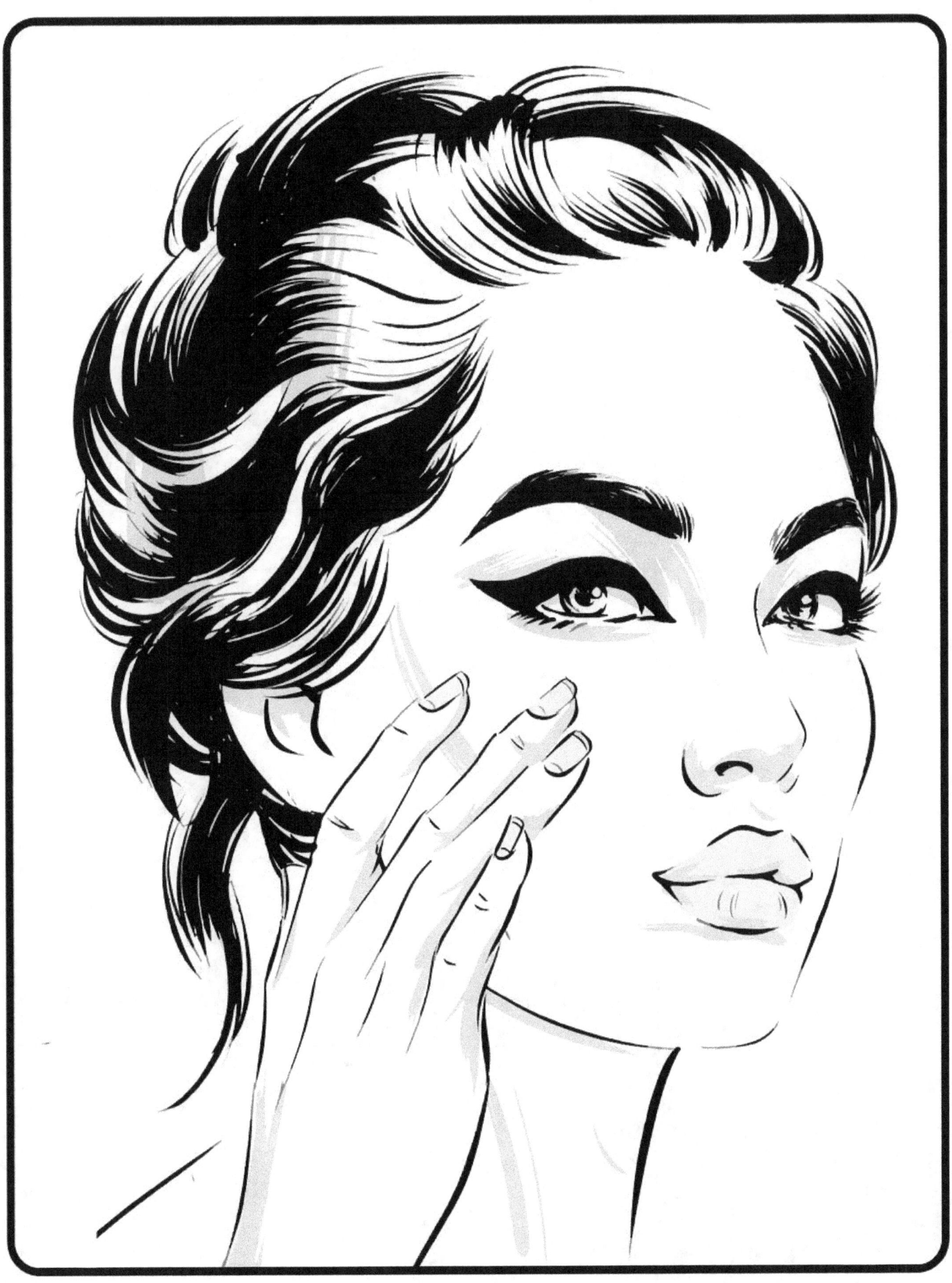

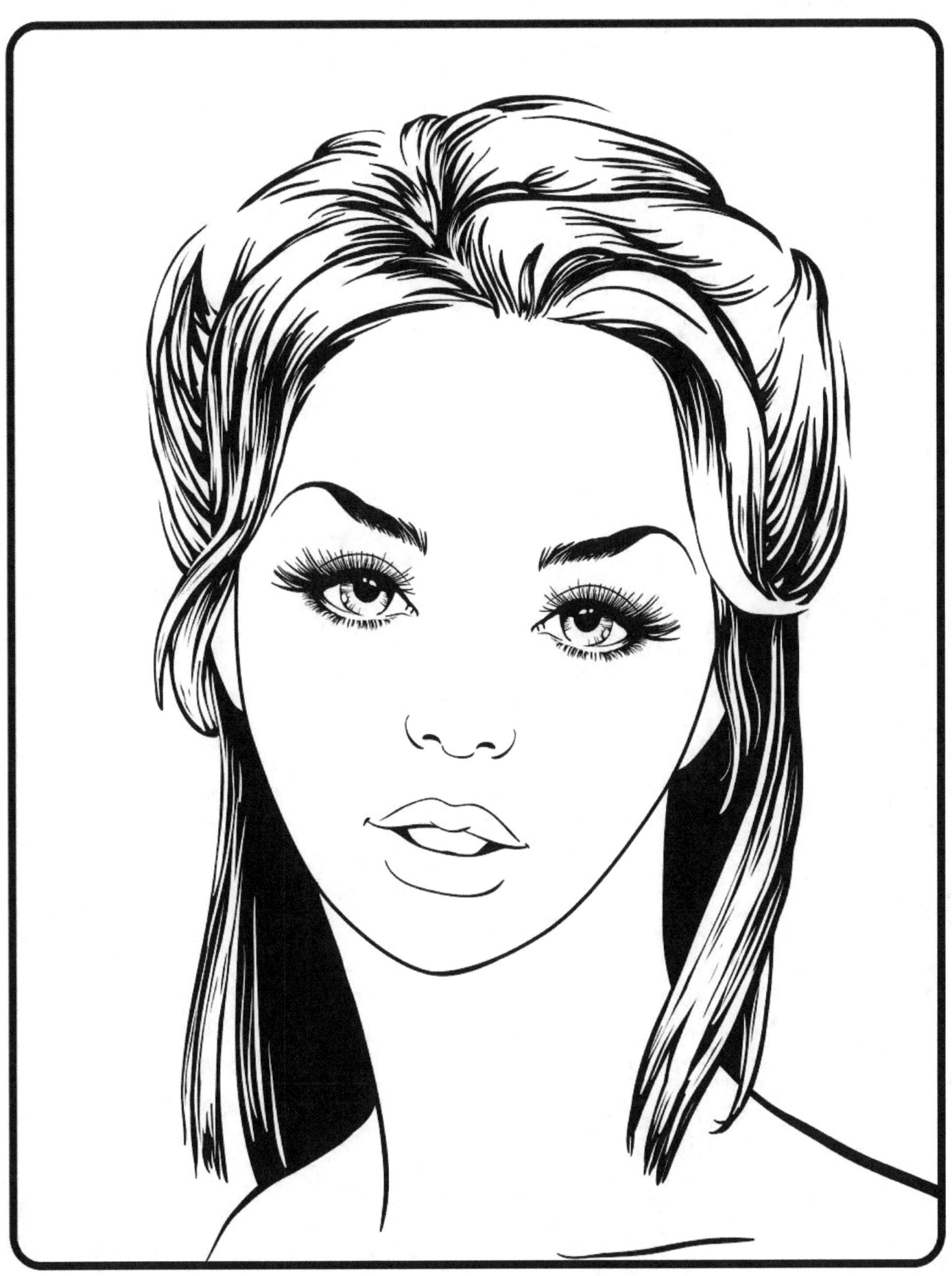

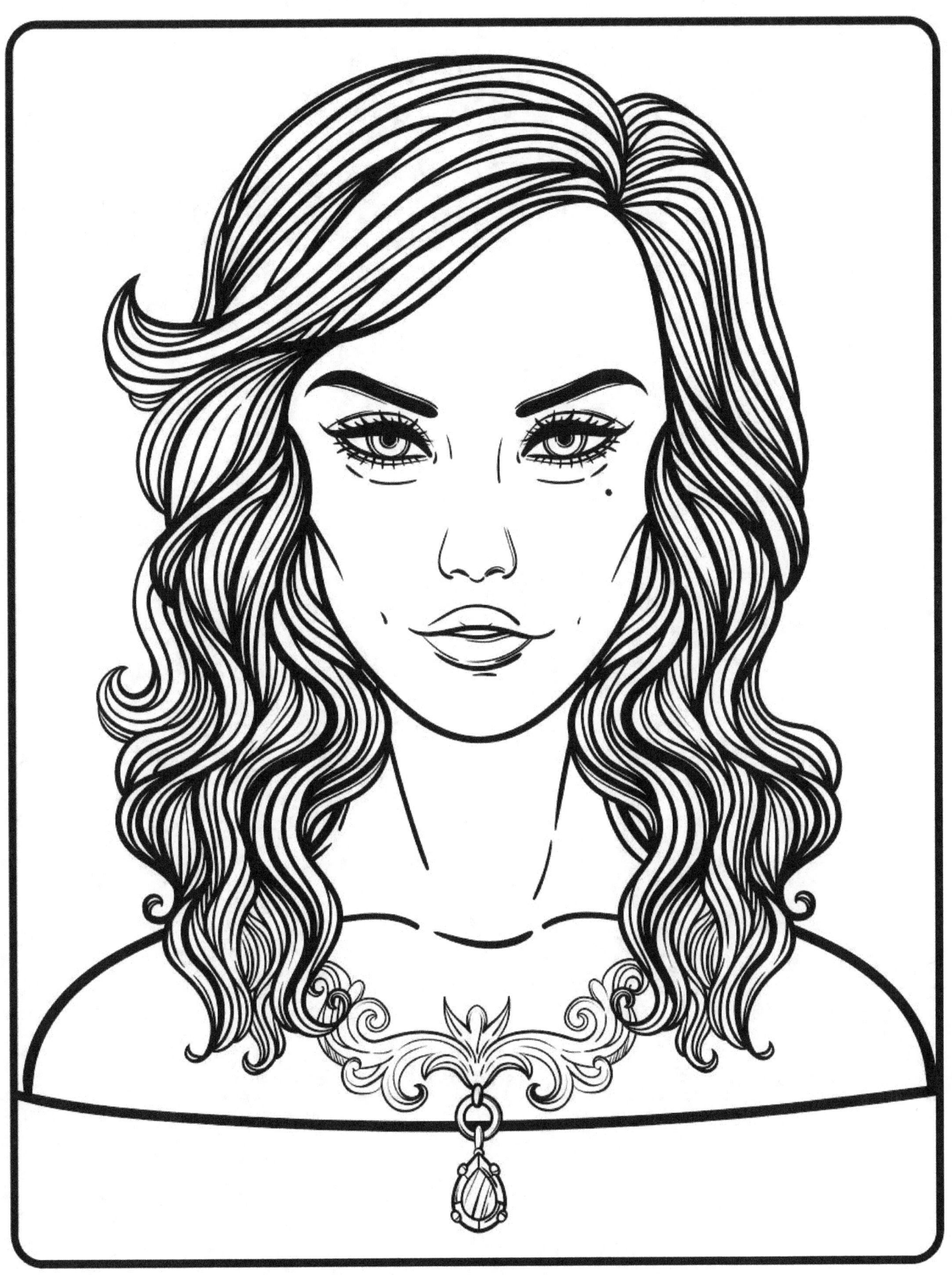

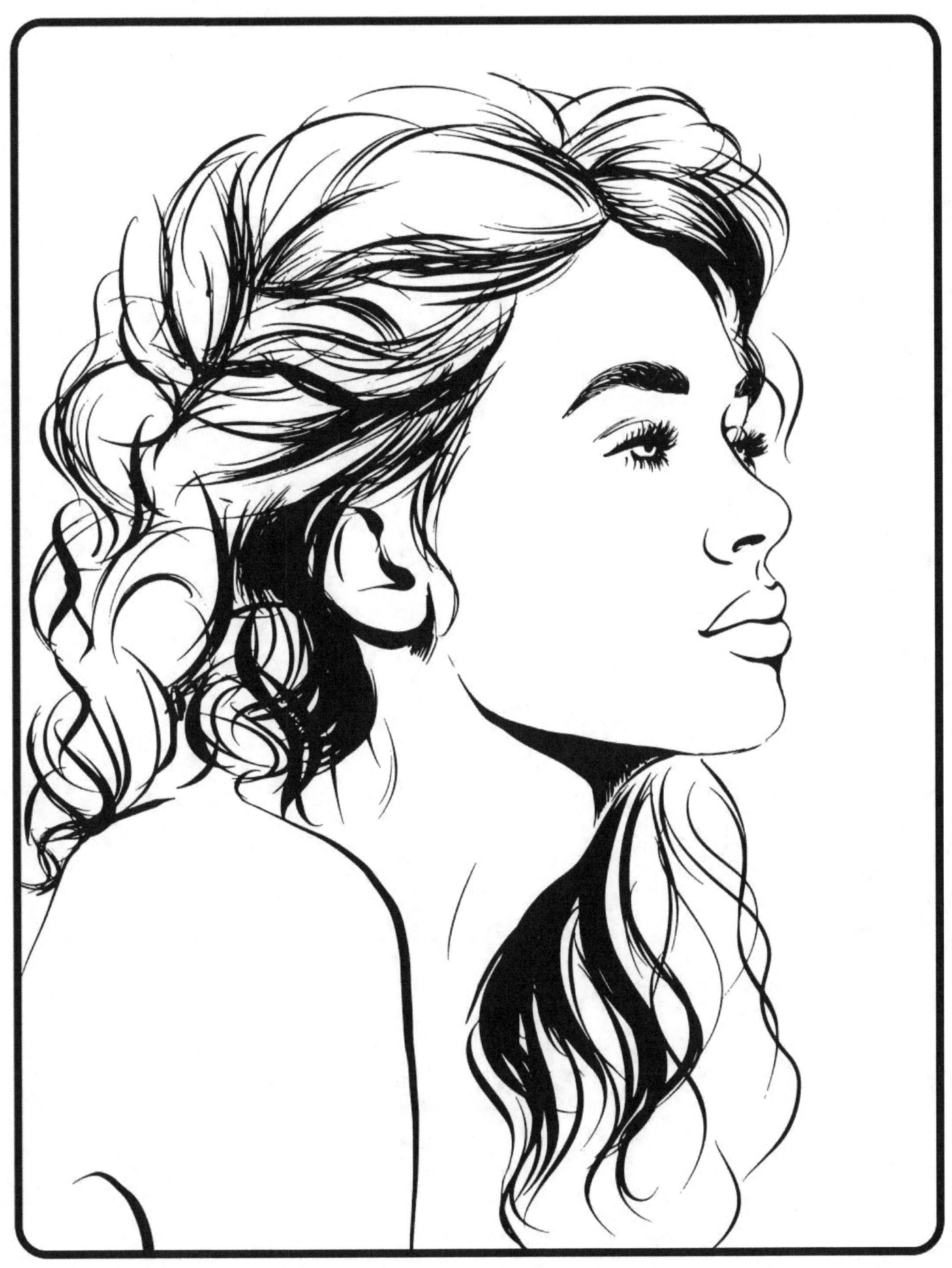

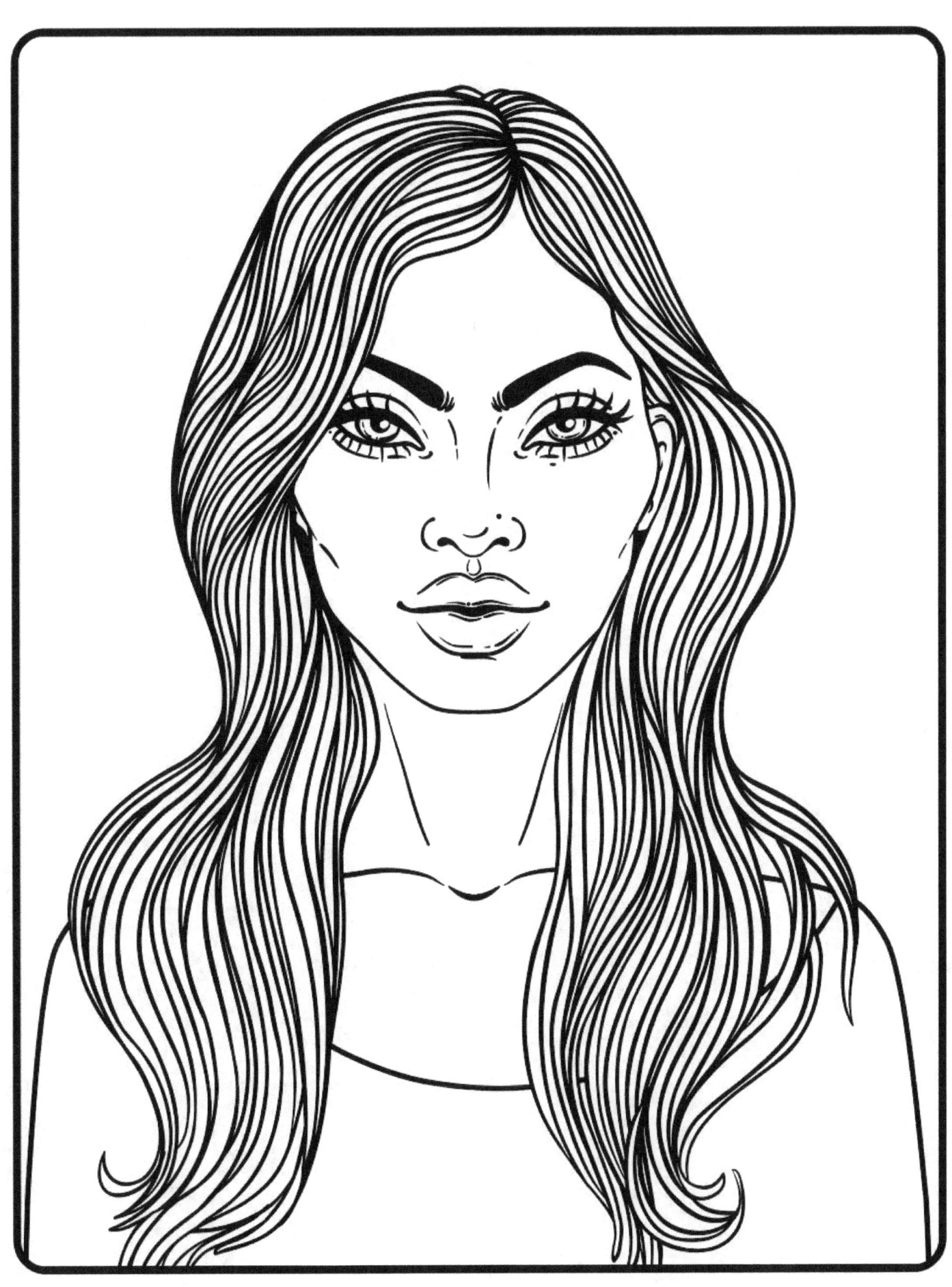

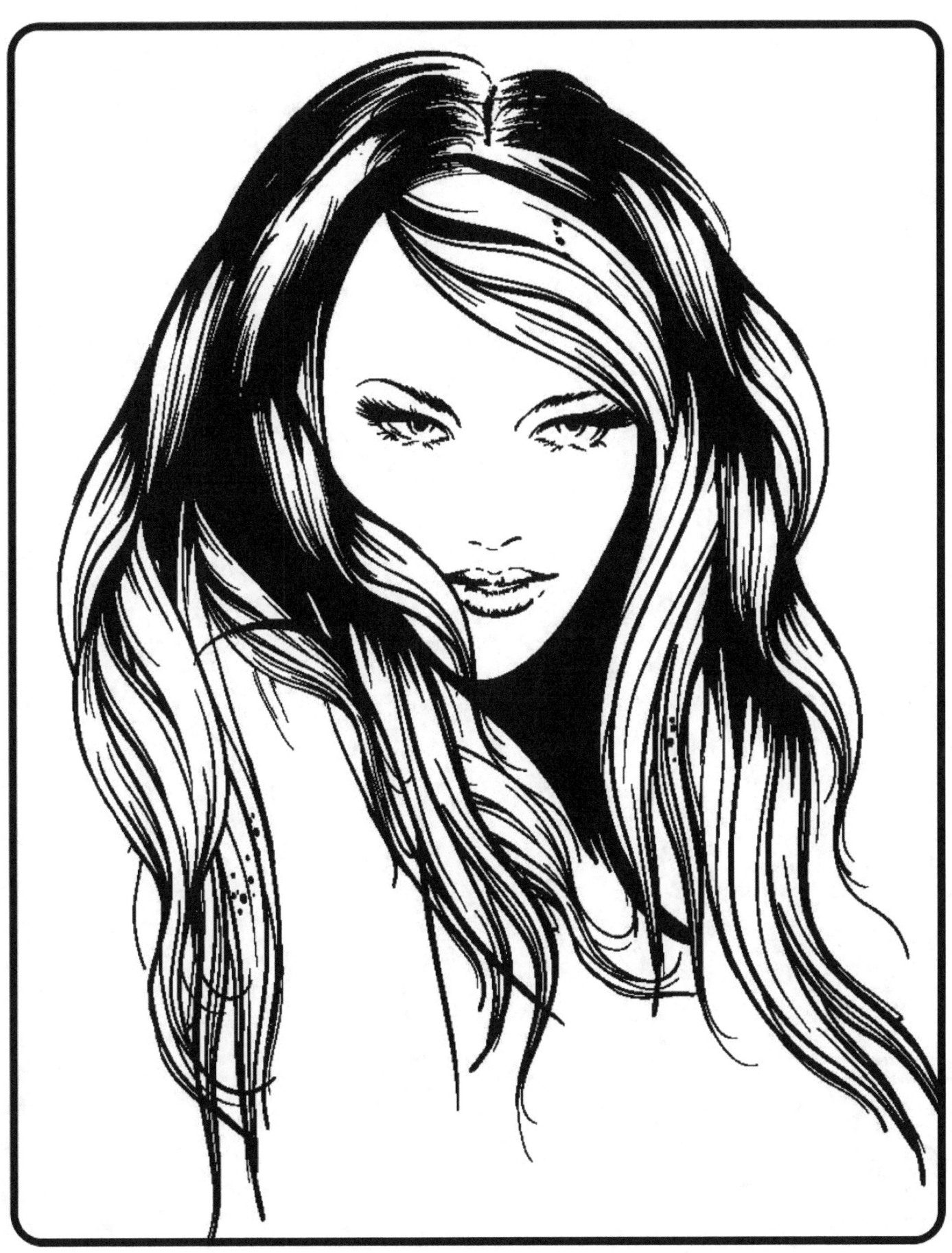

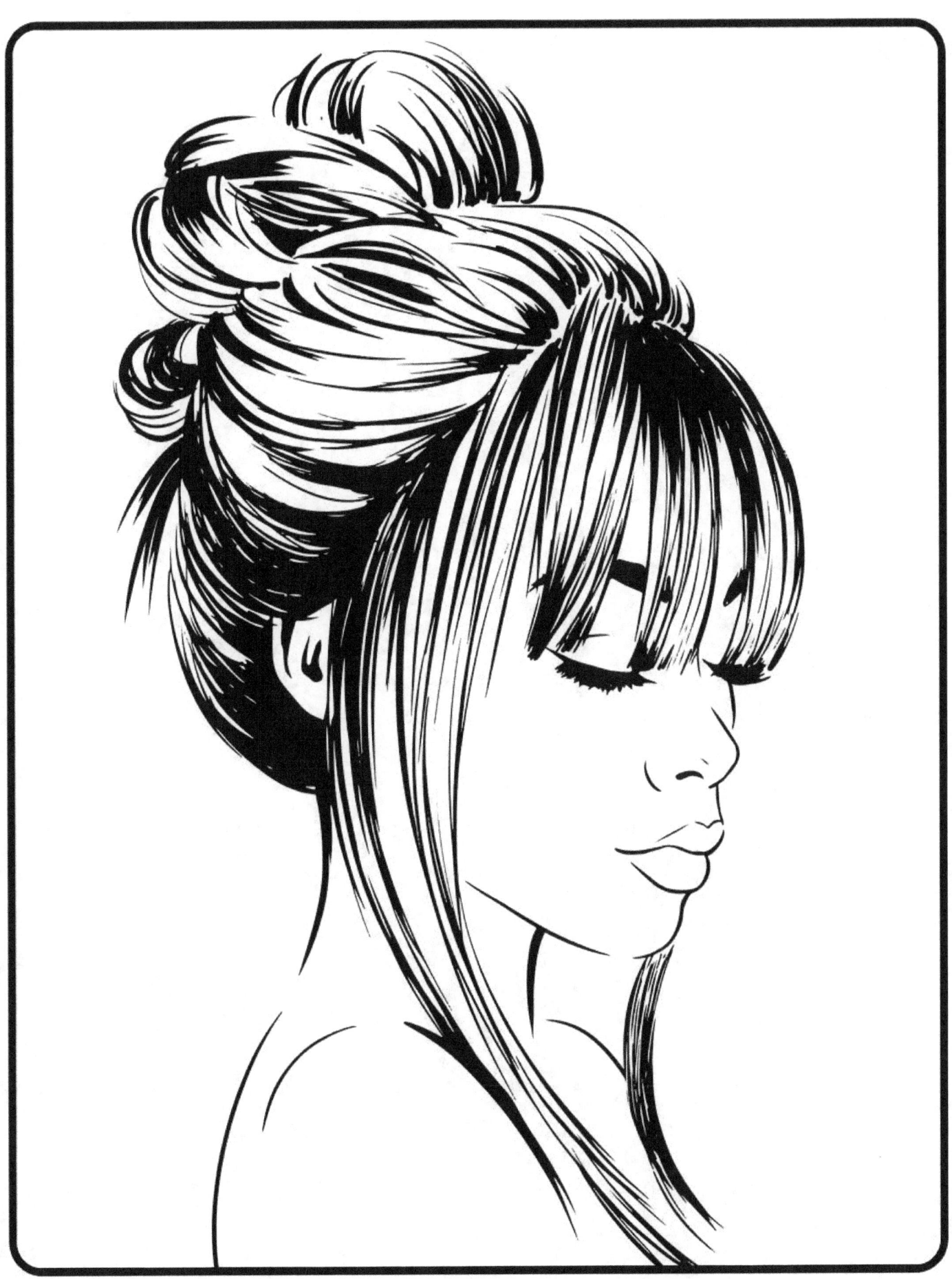

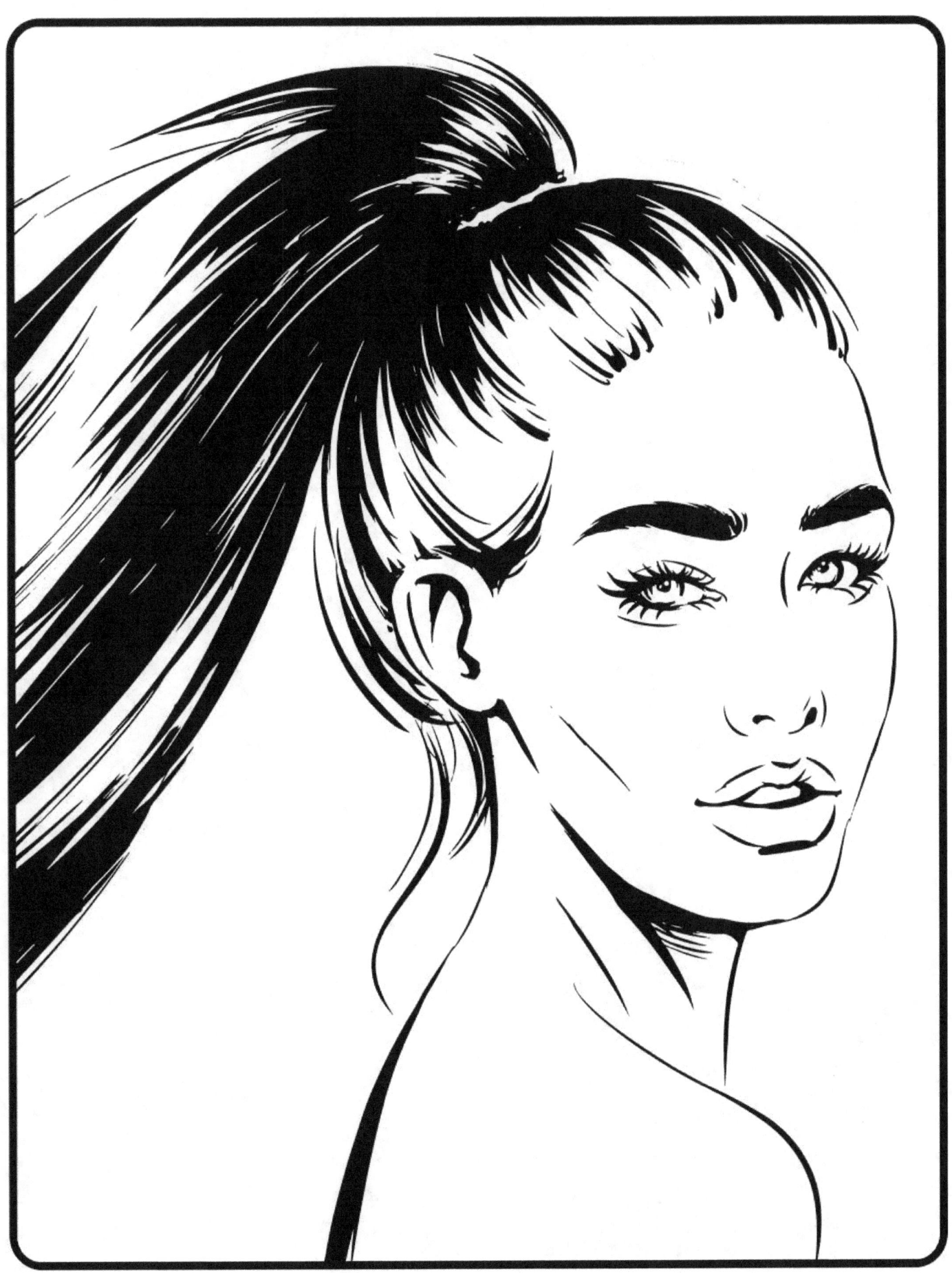

More coloring books from Katrin Stark

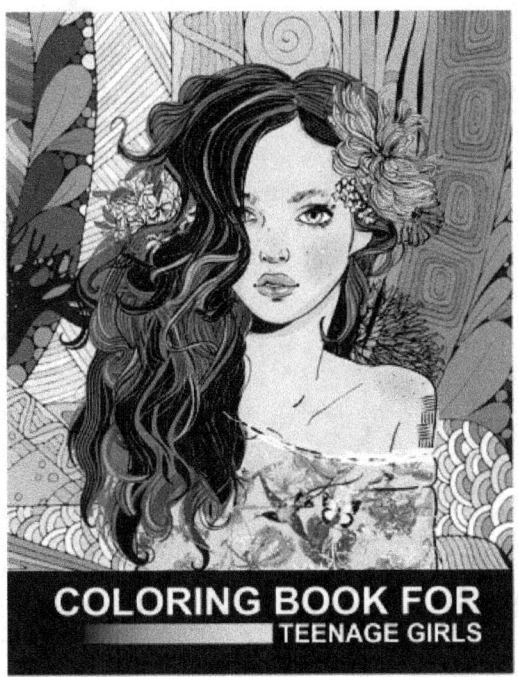
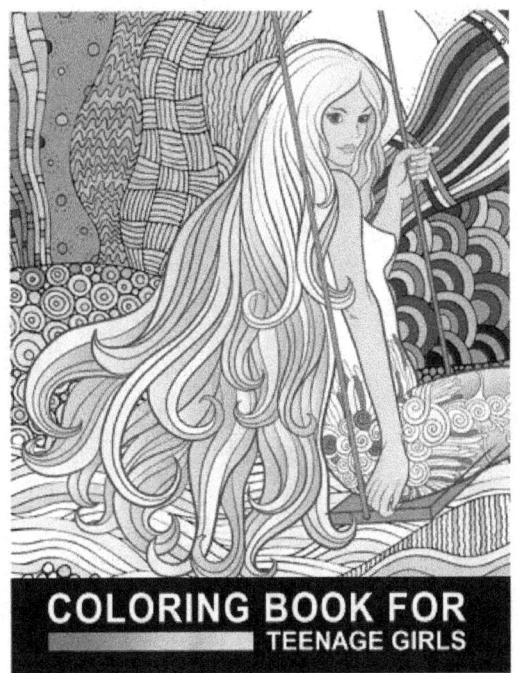
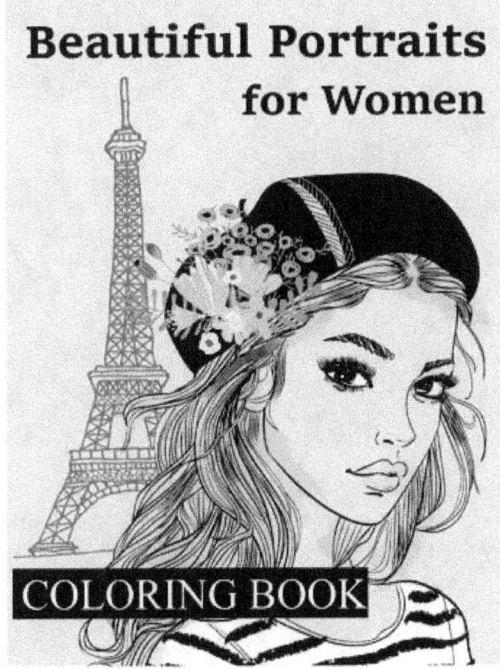
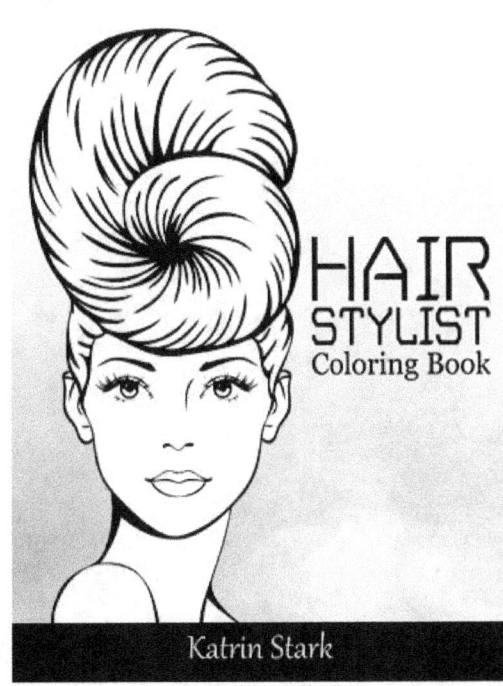

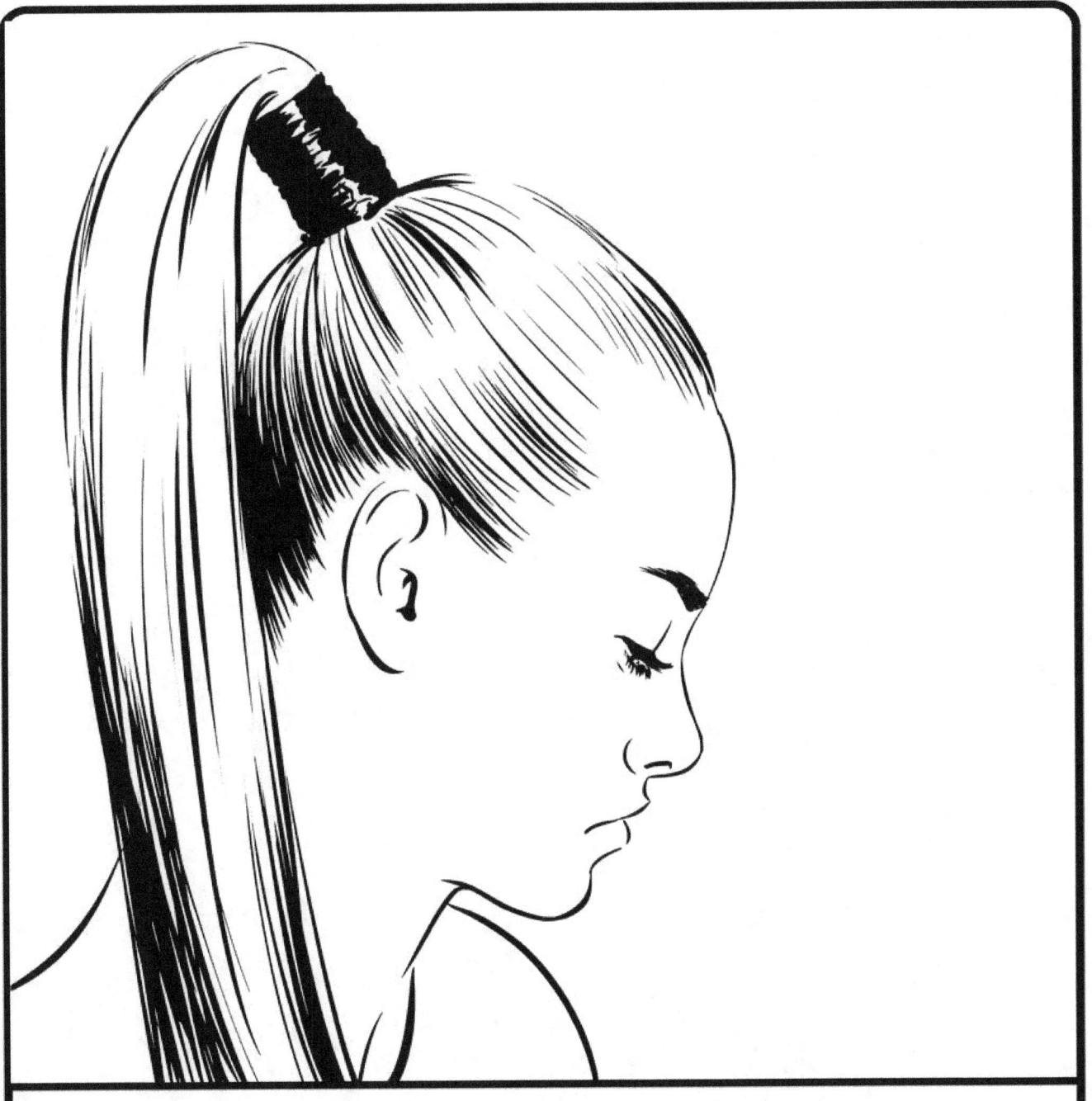

Thank you for buying this book

If you like the book, please consider leaving a review,
it will help author to create better books in the future

www.amazon.com/Katrin-Stark
www.amazon.co.uk/Katrin-Stark